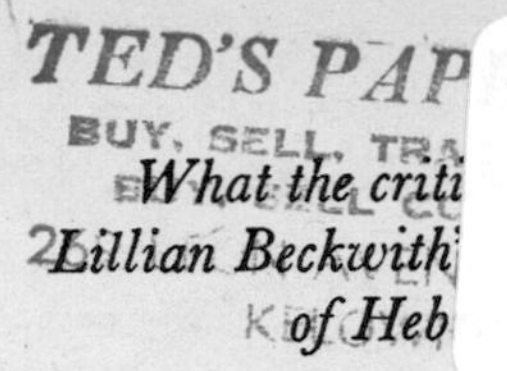

What the criti
Lillian Beckwith
of Heb

THE HILLS IS LONELY

'A bouquet for Miss Beckwith. . . . She is a gallant woman, and has written with brio and delight' Eric Linklater, *John O'London's*

THE SEA FOR BREAKFAST

'Hilarious. . . . I haven't laughed so much since *Whisky Galore*' Maurice Wiggin, *Sunday Times*

A ROPE – IN CASE

'As delightfully and unsentimentally drawn as ever' *Sunday Times*

LIGHTLY POACHED

'A beautiful book this, smelling of earth and sea, carrying the atmosphere of the crofts, and forcing you to laugh aloud' *Oxford Mail*

BEAUTIFUL JUST!

'Its humour is happy, easy and natural' *Daily Mirror*

Also in Arrow by Lillian Beckwith

About My Father's Business
The Bay of Strangers
Beautiful Just!
Green Hand
The Hills is Lonely
Lightly Poached
The Loud Halo
A Proper Woman
A Rope — In Case
The Sea for Breakfast
A Shine of Rainbows

The Hebridean Omnibus

LILLIAN BECKWITH

Bruach Blend

Decorations by
DOUGLAS HALL

ARROW BOOKS

Arrow Books Limited
20 Vauxhall Bridge Road, London SW1V 2SA

An imprint of Random Century Group

London Melbourne Sydney Auckland
Johannesburg and agencies throughout
the world

First published by Hutchinson 1978
Arrow edition 1980
Reprinted 1982, 1984, 1985, 1986, 1988 and 1990

Printed and bound in Great Britain by
Courier International Ltd, Tiptree, Essex

ISBN 0 09 921940 9

Contents

1	Spring Cleaning	9
2	Pets and Pests	27
3	'Lovely Bully'	43
4	Fisherman Willy	62
5	A 'Right Ceilidh'	79
6	Infernal Gulliver	91
7	Tinker Tales	115
8	Rowan	137
9	The Mirror	150
10	Christmas Sabbath	170

This book is dedicated to all my friends

Vocabulary

Cailleach	Old woman	Kyle-yak
Bodach	Old man	Bodak
Mo ghaoil	My dear	Mo gale
Ceilidh	An impromptu meeting for gossip and song	Cayley
Strupak (ch)	A cup of tea and a bite to eat	Stroopak
Oidhche mhath!	Good night!	Oi she-va
Potach	Oatmeal mixed with water and pressed into a ball or cake	Pot-ak
Sooyan	A young coalfish	Soo-yan
Mor	Big or tall	Mor
Beag	Small	Vic
Prapak	A very small haycock	Pra-pak
Tonag	Broad-bottomed	To-nag
Ruag	Red	Roo-ag
He Fooar!	It is cold!	Hay-foo-ar
Glic	Wise	Glic
Fear an tighe	Master of ceremonies	Fear-an-tie
Poc	A bag or sack	Pok

The approximate pronunciation of the name 'Tearlaich' is 'Charlac'.

A 'Tystie' (pronounced 'tisty') is a guillemot.

I

Spring Cleaning

It was such a good-looking day; blue-skied and smiling with sunshine; tuneful with sandpipers, and with a shimmering breeze stirring the sea into foam-tipped ripples which, as they reached the shore, rose to throw themselves over the sharp-pointed rocks like white hoopla rings. The sea itself was busy with gannets diving, terns swooping and splashing and tysties bobbing, while between the outer islands there emerged the shapes of homeward-bound fishing boats, mistily distorted as if one was seeing them through fogged glass.

On the Bruach crofts early orchis grew sturdily among the struggling new grass, and in the boggy hollows infant reeds speared fresh and green above the scythe-beheaded tussocks of the previous year. There were still snow-filled corries among the dark hills, but as each day the light lengthened by 'a hen's stride' the moors shed more and more of their winter brown like a partial moult, revealing patches of new spring green. The Bruach sheep stock, still heavy with lamb, fed greedily, indifferent to the honking ravens chaperoning their new brood; to the reciprocal calling of cuckoos and to the discursive twitterings of larks and pipits which were only now seeking suitable nesting sites.

May in Bruach was usually a good month, providing us with at least a few days of sun and calm, but this year the spell of good weather had come exceptionally early. Already the peats were cut and lying beside the bog awaiting the hot June sunshine which, hopefully, would dry them to almost coal-like solidness; the potatoes had been planted and the oats sown and now we awaited the first green spikes of corn and the dark green leaves of the potatoes to appear above the soil. The byres had been cleaned; and the cattle had been de-loused, an undertaking which is not so disagreeable as it sounds since we merely shook louse-powder prodigally all over the cows, particularly in the area of the neck and behind the ears where the lice were most likely to breed, and rubbed it in vigorously. Then, as Erchy put it, 'We could just watch the spiteful wee buggers go mad with their dyin'.'

Outdoor work being so well advanced I, like my neighbours, was indulging in the usual frenzy of spring cleaning. Doormats which had been caked with winter mud had been beaten and were now lying well weighted down with boulders in the burn. Upstream of the doormats lay the hearth and bedroom rugs, similarly weighted, and there I intended they should stay until the swift-flowing water had restored the doormats to their normal ginger-brown shagginess and the hearth and bedroom rugs looked as if they had just come back from the cleaners. The earth dykes around my croft were draped with sheets bleaching in the sun; newly washed blankets hung from the clothes rope where they responded to the caress of the breeze which, as it dried them, teased their fibres into downy softness and filled them with the good fresh smell of pure Highland air.

Perhaps because sunshine is scarcer in the Hebrides we tended to assess its qualities seriously. Thus May was traditionally the best month for bleaching and blanket washing. The hot summer sun, if and when it came, was welcome for drying the peats, but it turned woollen blankets yellow and hurried the drying of linen. To bleach successfully one needed the slow-drying, spring sunshine. A sheet put out to bleach in June or July would need to be sluiced frequently with clean water to ensure it did not dry too quickly, and as clean water had to be carried from the well it was far too precious a commodity for such ministrations. So we made the most of any good May weather, leaving the spread sheets out over several days and nights to be soaked repeatedly by the abundant May dew and subsequently dried by its benign sunshine. When the time came to gather them in, even the most obstinate stains had disappeared and the sheets were almost eye-dazzling in their whiteness.

Such knowledge I had of course acquired since living and working with the Bruach crofters, for once they realized I was in earnest they were eager enough to teach me not just the essentials I needed to know and practise to survive the crofting life but the simpler more esoteric crofting lore. One of the most important things I had to learn was how to be 'kind to myself' when lifting and carrying the many loads which in Bruach had to be carried on one's back because there was no other means of transportation. So well versed did I consider myself in this particular skill that, while visiting a mainland art gallery, I found myself looking appreciatively at Caravaggio's *Christ Bearing the Cross* and musing with irreverent practicality, 'He's not being kind to himself carrying it like that . . . A crofter could have shown him a much easier way of doing it. . . .' By precept and example, sometimes by good-natured mocking of my mistakes, the crofters continued to teach me, and undoubtedly the assimilation of their tutoring enabled me to adapt far more easily to the crofting life than I might otherwise have done.

It was late in the afternoon now, time to give the

hens their evening mash and almost time to begin preparing my own meal. But though it was not croft work I was involved with at the moment, I was loath to leave the task of giving the final coat of paint to a newly acquired but very second-hand chest of drawers which I had bought some time previously at a mainland auction and which I was refurbishing, ready to go into the spare bedroom. The bedroom itself was presently empty of furniture save for the bed, which had already been painted *in situ*, and the mattress which was reared on its side sunning itself before the wide-open window. The walls and ceiling had been repainted in a colour scheme of bluc and white, and tomorrow I planned to scrub the floor and put everything back in place, re-hang the fresh-laundered curtains, replace the sun-bleached white bedspread and move in the newly painted chest of drawers. The rugs would not be dry for some days, but by then the room should be well aired and free from the smell of paint, ready for the rugs to go down and ready for the visitors I was soon expecting.

The chest had already been rubbed down and given its first two coats of paint while it was in the barn where it had stood since the carrier had delivered it, but rather than risk it being marred by hayseeds or chaff I had brought it into the porch of the cottage for its final painting. I wielded my brush as painstakingly as time permitted, working into joints and crevices, covering up the last traces of its life of abuse, and when I stood up, the painting finished, I was pleased enough with the result. After putting away the tin of paint, I went round to the back of the cottage where I wiped the paintbrush first on a boulder and then more thoroughly on a patch of rough grass before immersing it in a jar of turpentine. That done, I wiped my paint-sticky hands on a turpentine-soaked rag and, bending down, likewise cleaned my hands on the grass. This was another simple crofter trick: another way of saving water and paper and even rags, all of which were scarce in Bruach. As much as possible one used grass for cleaning, but even so one did not pull up a bunch of grass to clean one's hands; one simply dragged them several times through the growing grass, which was not only a much easier and quicker method of cleaning but an infinitely more effective one. The only time a crofter pulled grass for cleaning was when he was using it as toilet paper.

Going into the kitchen I prepared the mash for the hens, and while thus engaged I heard a flapping of wings and the questioning cluck of a hen. Turning quickly to investigate, I saw to my utter dismay that Blackie, one of the tamer members of my flock of poultry, had become impatient for her evening feed and had escaped from the hen run. She had made her way to the door of the cottage where, no doubt hearing the telltale sounds of mash being mixed and wanting to urge on the proceedings, she had flown up on top of my newly painted chest and was even now stamping it with the skimble-skamble of her feet.

I shouted and lunged towards her, brandishing the wooden mixing spoon, and with a panic-stricken squawk she flew outside, shedding several of her feathers as she did so. In her wake the black feathers floated lazily down to settle on the wet paint. I picked them off, silently inveighing against the despoiler and against my own mismanagement, since if I had not kept the hens waiting for their mash it was unlikely Blackie would have become so impatient. Though the feathers had left barely a trace on the paintwork the top of the chest was in a fearful mess and I decided that the best thing to do was to try and brush out the marks as quickly as possible before the paint began to dry. With this in mind I rushed off to the hen run, gave the hens their feed, ensured they were all safely penned in behind the wire netting, rushed back to the house and took up my paintbrush once more. My own meal would have to wait until the painting was finished, just as Bonny would have to wait to be milked and given her reward of a potach. I set to work with resolute haste and again when I had finished I was not too dissatisfied with the result, though Blackie's skidding claws had marked the chest with easily perceptible scratches which I knew ought to have been left to dry and then rubbed down with sandpaper before being repainted. But I could not face the thought of starting the whole process again. Already I was beginning to begrudge the time it had all taken, since by temperament I am a slap-happy painter just as I am slap-happy at most tasks, always wanting to get them done with speed rather than skill or, as my grandmother used to reprove me, 'Always in too much of a rush to get a job jobbed.'

Belatedly I set about preparing my own meal and ate it while listening to the radio. The weather forecasters promised us a calm, dry spell, so confirming the portents of the evening sky, and mentally I listed how many of the more urgent jobs I should be able to get 'jobbed' before the fine spell came to an end.

After a leisurely cup of coffee I got out the wash-bowl, filled it with hot water from the kettle and washed my few supper dishes. A midge settled on my bare arm and I annihilated it with a sharp slap. But then there was another and yet another. Damn! I thought. It was just my luck that the breeze which all day had kept the midges at bay had apparently now dropped away completely, which meant I should have to make my way through swarms of the little pests when I went out on the moors to milk Bonny. Though I kept a supply of anti-midge lotion handy, no matter how lavishly it was applied the voracious midges could always find some area of flesh that was insufficiently protected.

I put the dishes away, concealing them in a cup-board, for much as I liked to have my china dis-played on the dresser I had found it too costly and too difficult to keep replacing dishes which were rattled from their places and shattered when, as frequently happened, the cottage door was either blown or flung open allowing the gale to thrash its way in. It was with a feeling of tired resignation that I slipped on my old milking coat, tied it as always with a short length of rope and picked up the milk pail and the stick I should need to dis-courage the more aggressive cows from coming too close in the hope of sharing Bonny's potach. It had been a long day and full of work and, there being a promise of good listening on the wireless that evening, I was planning to relax for a couple of hours' knitting and listening before it was time for bed. At this time of year the cattle were all out on the moors and as I closed the kitchen door behind me I was hoping Bonny would not have wandered too far from the crofts so I should not have to waste time looking for her. The cottage door was still open as I had left it when I had finished painting and as I glanced at the chest in passing both pail and stick dropped from my hands.

'Oh, no!' I groaned aloud. 'Oh, no!' I repeated, and stood staring dejectedly at the chest. How could I have been so stupid? Why, oh why, when the first midge had settled on my arm had I not instantly realized that if the midges were coming through the open window into the kitchen then they would most certainly be coming through the open door into the porch? Now the proof of their invasion was plain enough; the pale blue paint was speckled all over with thousands and thousands of tiny black midges. I glowered at the ruined paintwork. There was nothing else for it now but to leave the paint to dry thoroughly and then begin again the process of stripping and sandpapering and painting. Even I, expert as I am in disguising shoddy workmanship, could see no alternative course. Bitterly disappointed I again picked up the milk pail and the stick. At that moment a figure appeared in the doorway.

'Why, Miss Peckwitt, but you look as cross as if you'd just cacced in nettles,' Tearlaich greeted me compassionately.

The days when I might have been embarrassed or even shocked by Tearlaich's remark had long since passed. Now, tired and angry and dejected though I felt, the innocent indelicacy of his greeting triggered off a bubble of laughter that rose and then exploded, making me shake with mirth. I was accustomed to the forthright earthiness of many of the Bruachites but Tearlaich was frequently so artlessly apt that even when stirred to eulogy he usually managed it with consummate impropriety.

'Tearlaich!' I chided him, still gurgling with laughter. 'The things you say!'

'It's true enough,' he retorted. 'It's the way you looked, just.'

'Maybe I did,' I conceded. 'But I'm sure no one else would have thought of saying it.' His eyes widened with pretended surprise. 'Anyway,' I went on, 'I had something to look upset about,' and I showed him the chest with its cargo of midges and explained that this was the second time within a couple of hours that disaster had struck.

'Ach, that's a shame, right enough,' he commiserated. 'Can you no paint over the beasties all the same? It would look kind of different.'

I grimaced. 'Too different.'

'Then touch them up with that brush of Ian's an' some different coloured paint. It would look as if it was meant then. Kind of stippled, they call it.'

I shook my head emphatically. There had been a brief outbreak of stippling in Bruach when Ian Mor had returned from a visit to Glasgow and brought with him a stippling brush which he declared was a quick and attractive way of decorating the walls of a room. Despite his mother's protestations he had set about stippling the smoke-darkened wood of their kitchen with bright green paint. Some people admired the result but I found the impact of the room made me almost gasp, as if I was in danger of drowning in a weed-covered pond. Fortunately the outbreak was limited to only two or three homes but even these were quickly masked with plain colours once it was known that the missionary had given his opinion that he thought it frivolous.

For a moment or two Tearlaich and I looked steadily at the chest as if waiting for a flash of inspiration.

'Aye, well, you're lucky,' he said at last.

'Lucky?'

'Aye, indeed you are so. See how many thousands of midges you have trapped there that can no longer take a bite out of you.' He took a piece of paper out of his pocket and handed it to me. 'Here you are,' he said, 'here's the receipt for your croft rent an' I'm tellin' you maybe next year you won't find a one that's keen to take it for you.' He sounded disgruntled, and as I glanced at him enquiringly my mind registered the fact that for a rent day he was surprisingly sober.

Bruach croft rents were paid annually in the spring when the factor left his office in the town and came to the estate manager's house to preside over the collection. In Bruach the paying of rent was regarded as being in the nature of a ceremony and since rent days, like burials and calf castrations, were exclusively male occasions and as such ended with the reward of a good dram of whisky, there was always a noticeable degree of elation in the air despite the fact that the crofters were being called upon to part with a relatively meagre portion of their carefully hoarded cash.

Leaving the women behind, the men, dressed in their best clothes but taking their cattle sticks and their dogs along with them, set out in groups to walk the six miles to the manager's house where at a white-scrubbed table in the kitchen they handed over their dues to the factor. In return for each croft rent they paid they were given a dram of whisky with which to drink the health of the absent laird. If a man paid the rent for a single croft he received only one dram but a man paying the rent for two or three crofts would be able to toast the laird accordingly. Not surprisingly, therefore, there was never any shortage of volunteers to deputize for any invalids or widows who either could not undertake or were tacitly discouraged from undertaking the twelve-mile walk.

I thanked Tearlaich and put the receipt away in a drawer. 'Dare I ask how many other rents you paid today?' I grinned at him.

'Amn't I after payin' eight of them?' he replied indignantly. 'The most I've ever paid an' here was me thinkin' what a fine happy fellow I'll be likely when I get home. I took an empty bottle with me this time, thinkin' to myself I'd take only two, maybe three drams at the manager's house an' have the rest put into the bottle to drink with the lads on the way home. Ach, but that bugger of a factor.' His voice grew bitter. 'They're tellin' me he's made it a rule that it's to be no more than one dram for a man no matter how many rents he pays.' Tearlaich's expression was one of outrage. 'I couldn't believe it at first. The manager gave me my first dram as he always does but then when I handed back the empty glass for him to fill it up he shook his head just an' made signs behind the factor's back. When I got the manager to himself for a minute I asked him what was the matter an' showed him the bottle I'd brought. He said he daren't give me more because the new factor had made this rule an' now he had to keep to it.'

Tearlaich paused to scrutinize my expression, no doubt assessing whether I was registering a suitable degree of shock. Satisfied, he allowed himself to continue, 'Indeed the old folk would be turnin' in their graves if they knew. Such a thing never happened in this place till now.'

I murmured consolingly, 'He's going to upset more folks than you.'

Tearlaich ignored my remark. 'I mind there was a factor came once that tried waterin' the whisky in the bottles before we got our drams. Now I ask you, Miss Peckwitt, what would be the use of watered whisky to a Bruach man? A man that knows poor whisky as quick as he knows there's a hayseed in his eye? Aye,' he continued, his resentful expression giving way to one of grim satisfaction, 'but we were a match for that one. We made it up among ourselves that instead of goin' in to pay our rent one at a time an' havin' a few words of chat we'd kind of make a queue, one directly behind the other, so there wasn't a chance for the bottles of whisky to be moved from the table once they were opened. Not with all those eyes watchin' there wasn't.' He ended with a grunt of malevolent laughter.

'And what happened the next year?' I asked.

'Ach, we got our whisky neat as ever an' nothin' said. He didn't try them tricks again.'

'Then maybe the factor was aware how you all felt this year and next year you won't be limited to one dram.'

'Damty sure we won't,' returned Tearlaich emphatically. 'We'll find some way of bestin' him. We're no doin' without our proper drams.'

'You and your whisky,' I challenged him. 'I believe you think more of whisky than you do of religion.'

'As much as anyway,' he retorted. 'An' why wouldn't I? There's things whisky can do for you that no religion can do.'

'Such as?' I prompted.

'Such as take the fire out of a fever; the ache out of lovin' an' the meanness out of a miser. Tell me anythin' else that will do that now.' But of course I couldn't. 'We think that much of whisky I reckon we ought to have our own blend of it. Bruach Blend. What would you think of that now?'

I smiled. 'It's occurred to me, Tearlaich,' I said, 'You may be blaming the factor when it isn't his fault at all. Whisky costs so much nowadays the laird himself may have imposed this new rule.'

He snorted. 'I doubt the laird doesn't know a thing about it,' he replied. 'The man's always provided a dram for every croft so why would he be stoppin' now? How would he be after knowin' that all the crofters aren't goin' to come an' pay their own rents?' His voice became suspicious. 'An' where does all the undrunk whisky go, d'you think? Back into the laird's stores?' We exchanged dubious glances. 'Ach, I'll tell you one thing for sure,' he asserted. 'This new factor we have is no gentleman. Not to my way of thinkin' he's not.'

Since coming to Bruach I had worked out that to qualify for the description 'gentleman' a man had to be liberal in the bestowal of whisky. Thus the laird qualified in his absence. He would have been even more highly regarded had he been present to drink alongside his tenants though the undertaking would doubtless have been a formidable one. In much the same way a woman qualified as a 'lady' if she graciously provided whisky in return for any help or favour she might receive from a crofter, the difference then being that if she drank along with him she would more likely have been regarded as a 'cow'.

Being neither 'lady' nor 'cow' I had no whisky in the house to offer Tearlaich, and as the only recompense for taking my rent and suffering what he lugubriously regarded as the factor's ill-usage I could only offer him a glass of my home-made bramble wine. He accepted with some caution but after one sip he drained the glass at a gulp.

'My God! You wouldn't dare put that in a baby's bottle,' he complimented me and accepted another glass. His glance fell on the milk pail. 'You're away to milk your cow then?'

'I am,' I told him, glancing not at the clock but at the sun which was making its languid way towards the peaks of the hills. 'It's high time I was away too.'

'Indeed then, you're in for a long walk,' he told me. I looked at him, hoping he was teasing, but my spirits sank when I saw no trace of a smile on his face. 'I was seein' your cow over the other side of the strath a wee while ago an' I'm thinkin' from the look of her she'll be there yet.'

The strath was about three miles away across the moors. 'I wonder whatever has taken her over there?' I asked, but even before I had finished putting the question I knew the answer. Until that moment I had forgotten that 'Crumley', the Department of Agriculture bull which had spent the last two summers in Bruach siring all the calves, had arrived the day before from the mainland and had, as usual, been put off the lorry on the other side of the strath. The strategy of putting the bull so far away from the village was to give the animal a few days of peace and quiet in which to recover from the journey before he discovered the sex-starved cows of Bruach or, as was more likely, they discovered his presence. But such tactics were always thwarted by Bonny, who had developed a most uncowlike passion for Crumley which even the Bruach crofters found remarkable. Although there was an estate bull available Bonny would have none of him and indeed she showed no signs of coming into season until Crumley arrived in the vicinity. But the moment she winded him off she would go in pursuit and for the rest of the summer she and Crumley were rarely out of each other's sight. It was not just a mating, it was a love affair and when the autumn came and Crumley had to return to his quarters on the mainland Bonny's protesting 'moos' as she watched the lorry take him away were heart-rending.

'They behave more like humans,' observed Anna Vic with a laugh. 'I'm thinkin' you'll be glad when the Department of Agriculture send us another bull instead of Crumley. Maybe she'll not get so fond of the next one.'

Admittedly the 'affair of the heart' between Bonny and Crumley was inconvenient from the point that Bonny, having had two early calvings, would undoubtedly be calving early again next year and in Bruach, though the occasional early calving was allowable for a winter milk supply, the lateness of spring grass and the consequent sparsity of feeding made a succession of early calvings undesirable. Any crofter who allowed it to happen was considered to be guilty of a reckless disregard for the well-being of his animals.

I ought to have agreed wholeheartedly with Anna Vic's observation but Bonny's love for Crumley was so touching I could not really be sure that I would be glad when another bull was substituted.

'Did you not notice she was bullin' this mornin' when you saw her?' Tearlaich asked. I shook my head. I had not noticed presumably because I had no long experience in the detection of such conditions. However, on reflection, I remembered she had been a little restless when I milked her.

'Aye, well I doubt you'll be seein' your bed before sunrise,' he confirmed.

I shrugged my shoulders. 'I suppose I'd better

leave this stick behind me,' I said. 'People tell me a stick is like a red flag to Crumley.'

'Aye, he's cross right enough when he wants to be,' Tearlaich admitted. 'But, ach, I doubt you've any need to worry yourself. When Crumley's been with your cow for a while he's too shagged out to care.'

2

Pets and Pests

To go so far alone late at night to milk an amorous cow which was being closely attended by an equally amorous bull was by no means an inviting prospect but I knew I dared not entertain for a moment any idea of leaving Bonny unmilked. I had to go because if I missed milking her there was a risk of mastitis developing and, due largely to my ignorance, Bonny had nearly died with mastitis and other complications shortly after she had given birth to her second calf. I had nursed her successfully through that illness but I had no wish to repeat the experience. It had been a time of pain and suffering for Bonny and of anguished vigilance and nauseating toil for me. At the onset of her illness the vet, who, justifiably, regarded me as an empirical crofter, had given her no more than a slim chance of survival. 'She's pretty bad,' he had warned me brusquely. 'It's a pity you couldn't have got word to me sooner.' Censure threaded its way into his voice.

'The telephone wires were down after the gale,' I reminded him miserably.

'Aye.' His eyes appraised the general apathy of Bonny's appearance. 'It's a pity,' he repeated. 'She was a fine young beast right enough.' His use of the past tense was like a punch in the chest.

I swallowed hard before I could speak. 'I'll nurse her,' I was quick to assure him.

'Maybe, but even supposing I save the cow I haven't much hope of saving her udder and what use to you will be a milk cow without an udder?' His voice was crisply matter of fact. I stroked Bonny's neck while I listened to the vet giving me the cold hard facts, but my mind rebelled at the principal that because an animal can no longer perform the function for which it is bred it should therefore forfeit its life. I felt a brief flare of antagonism towards the vet. It was Bonny he was talking about, I wanted to remind him. Bonny who trusted me; who would come when I called; who would give me her milk as willingly as if I were her calf; who would stand contentedly allowing me to rest my binoculars on her back while I scanned the moors. Bonny, whose affectionate licking had to be endured even though her tongue was like a steel file on my flesh. Oh, she could be as cantankerous as any other cow at times but she was still my Bonny; the first cow I had ever had and I could not bear the thought of letting her die.

'I want you to try and save her,' I insisted.

I thought I detected a glimmer of sympathy in the vet's glance. 'Aye well, I'll do what I can,' he promised without much optimism. 'But what you must try to understand,' he went on to explain, 'is when a cow gets sick like this it more often than not just gives up without a fight. Very often I could cure the sickness in the beast but what kills them is the lack of will to live and there's nothing anybody can do about that.'

As he set about giving her a drench I vowed that not only would I nurse Bonny to the best of my strength and ability but I would also try by the force of my own will to instill in her the will to recover. For the next few days I spent most of my time in the byre, stroking and patting her; fondling her cold ears and talking to her, urging her to resist the fate which threatened her. Every hour or so I brought hot water from the house and bathed her fevered udder and subsequently, though my stomach retched and heaved as I performed the task, I regularly swabbed away the sloughing, stinking gangrenous flesh before massaging ointment into the exposed and bleeding rawness beneath. At night, overcoming my dread of insects and mice, I wrapped myself in blankets and lay on a bed of hay beside her stall, sleeping and half-sleeping and always conscious of her grunts and heavy breathing. Sometimes I wakened to the touch of her wet nose and her warm foetid breath as she explored my face or to the rasp of her rough confiding tongue on my hand. In response I murmured endearments and encouragement until her discomfort seemed to ease or until I had talked myself into an anxiety-ridden mockery of sleep. In the mornings, instead of feeling refreshed I was usually swaying with tiredness and my eyes grew so heavy with lack of sleep I feared my drooping eyelids were in danger of tripping me up as I walked. Perhaps it is the height of eccentricity to sleep with a cow but I believed she was comforted by my presence and I sensed that such a communion developed between us that when the time of crisis came she was sustained by my own determination that she should live.

The vet began to look less pessimistic and cautiously increased Bonny's chance of recovery to an even fifty-fifty. But then came the night I should never forget; the night when I was awakened by a sensation that I was being pushed out of bed and, sitting up, I discovered with a huge surge of elation that Bonny was not only up on her feet but eager for some of the hay which comprised my makeshift bed. She was determinedly pulling out choice mouthfuls of it from under my body. With a light heart I quickly vacated the bed and pushed the remaining hay into her manger. She ate greedily and before I left her to go for my own breakfast she was showing the most anxiously watched-for sign of recovery in a cow – she was chewing her cud!

When the vet next called I was able to greet him with a relieved smile. 'Thank you for pulling her through,' I said.

'Thank yourself,' he replied. 'You must have given her plenty of attention.'

I was tempted to tell him I had slept in the byre at night with Bonny but decided against it. He regarded me quizzically. 'Are you used to nursing?' he asked.

'Certainly not,' I denied. 'I've always regarded myself as being one of those "faint at the sight of blood" women. Far too squeamish to be a nurse.'

'Aye, that's what I thought,' he admitted. 'When you said about saving the cow I thought to myself the gangrene would be too much for you. It's a nasty job even for one that's accustomed to it.'

I did not tell him that the stench of it had made me feel so sick there were days when I could not eat because of it. I shrugged. 'It had to be done, didn't it?'

The vet seemed to be looking at me with a new respect. 'Aye,' he agreed, 'it had to be done and it seems it was worth it. After all,' he added, 'she still has half an udder.'

It was that pathetic half-udder I was now on my way to milk and as I made towards the strath where Tearlaich had reported seeing Bonny I allowed myself to think for a moment or two how comforting would have been the prospect of returning home after milking as I had planned earlier with nothing more demanding to do than a little knitting or sewing while listening to a radio play. I dismissed the thought before it made me discontented since with Bonny the other side of the strath I knew only too well that not only the play but the night's broadcasting would be finished before I could hope to get back. But of such upsets was the crofting life composed and though I feared I should never be able to accept them with the same tranquil philosophy as my neighbours I was aware that at last I was learning to limit my reactions to no more than lukewarm resentment.

The corncrakes were craking to one another among the rough grass where the croft land merged inconspicuously with the moors, and the moors themselves when I reached them were resonant with the sad, goat-like drumming of snipe. A gentle chill in the evening air had driven the midges back into their underworld among the grass and heather and I walked unmolested, enfolded in the blended sun-dried scents of bog myrtle and wild thyme, sedges, bedstraws and moss which fringed the path. The coolness lay against my hot sunburned cheeks like clean, well-pressed linen; the dew seeped invigoratingly through the openwork of my sandals; youthful bracken wiped my bare legs with fresh green fronds. Before me the familiar peaks of the hills were like enormous black thorns piercing the fiery sunset while below the faintly rippled loch was like a spread net which had caught the afterglow and was holding it as its prize. The flawless beauty of the scene was like an anodyne assuaging all tiredness and irritation and I abandoned myself to its all-encompassing serenity.

There were times when I thought that 'moors' was too gentle a term for the vast area of rock which surrounded the Bruach crofts. Treeless, fissured with peat bogs and smeared with a few tatters of vegetation they had a threadbare look like an old, abandoned carpet. Yet despite their austerity they were beautiful, abounding with shape and form and though they were drab there was nevertheless an enormous variety of colours concealed among the drabness. There were burns, too, rollicking down to the sea as only Highland burns can rollick, and sheltered corries, walled by rock slabs and floored not with soft grass but with springy turf crisp with bents and sedges. In the summer twilight the apparent severity was softened and the moors invested themselves with an almost tangible aura of mystery which made even the mundane trudge to milk a cow into a small adventure. Long acquaintance had not made me insensible of their mystery; indeed there were still times when I was almost frightened out of my wits by it but in general I had come to regard it as I regarded an illusionist trick; intriguing but explicable; compelling but not un-nerving. For example, I knew now that the cowled monk-like figure silhouetted against the skyline and seeming to block my path was in reality only a slim weather-chiselled pinnacle of rock which by day had no mysticality; that the human-sounding cough which might suddenly slash the heavy silence of a deserted corrie probably came from some old ewe which had temporarily forsaken the rest of the flock to seek a quiet refuge where she might give birth to her lamb; that the appreciative-sounding whistle which seemed to come from just behind my shoulder was likely to be the call of a golden plover flying low overhead and that the spine-chilling hissing close at hand would, on investigation, prove to be nothing more menacing than the dialogue between a couple of courting or combative hedgehogs.

I was accustomed to being alone on the moors at night, but as I picked my way now round the cowled monk I felt a sudden stab of apprehension, for there, hurrying towards me along the narrow track, was the figure of a man carrying a stick. I knew instantly from his gait that he was no Bruachite and since it was unusual because of the treacherously narrow paths for a stranger to be on the moors at this time I surmised immediately that there had been an accident to some climber in the hills and that this was either a hiker or a climber hurrying to get help. I stepped aside so as not to impede him and as he approached I realized he was neither a hiker nor a climber. To my astonishment I saw that he was wearing a town suit and that the 'stick' he was carrying was no stick but a furled umbrella. I was flabbergasted. An umbrella on the Bruach moors? With unashamed curiosity I watched him draw nearer and as I saw him more clearly I was struck by the pallor of his skin even in the evening light and by the cold glazed look in his eyes.

'Good evening,' I murmured, assuming he was English. But he ignored me and passed without a glance or a word, hurrying along the path as if he was both deaf and panic stricken, his eyes looking to neither left nor right and his brow deeply furrowed. For a moment I was aware of a prickle of disquiet but I dismissed it. Incongruous as he appeared, the man was real enough, of that I was certain, since there had been a detectable smell of stale tobacco about him as he passed me. But, I asked myself, why, garbed as he was and carrying an umbrella, was he out on the moors so late at night? Where had he come from? Why, since I am not a tiny waif-like creature who could easily melt into a background, had he passed me by so unseeingly? If he was a tourist why, oh, why on a night like this was he not dawdling, gloating on the incredibly beautiful sunset and yielding to its demand for adulation instead of hurrying as if to get away from it all? I pondered the incident for some time as I continued on my way, but realizing that I would only need to mention the man to Morag when I saw her for a perfectly rational explanation of his presence to be forthcoming, I shrugged away the thought of the hurrying man and dwelt on my own good fortune in not having to hurry anywhere at all. It mattered little to me that it would be well after midnight when I returned home from milking. I could always sleep late the next morning if my body demanded I should do so and thereafter I could work my day according to Bruach time, which was a time that only nuzzled at one gently, unlike city time, which has sharp teeth and gnaws endlessly at one's contentment. And if, because of the threatened change in the weather, there was some urgency about a task, then I should hurry in the Bruach way; not scurry, which again is the artificial and unnecessary hurry that city people like to indulge in and which I liked to think I had completely forsworn.

I planned, as I plodded on, that before I went to bed I should fill the hens' trough with food and so deter them from becoming too vociferously indignant as they undoubtedly would if their morning feed was late; and if, as I guessed would happen, too many opportunist gulls and crows, spying the full trough and no human being in attendance, grew confident enough to visit the hen run and steal a good proportion of the food then I would compensate the hens by giving them a larger feed in the evening. The slight departure from routine might cause them to retaliate by laying fewer eggs for a day or two but since it was the height of the egg-laying season they would still provide for my requirements. Perhaps I should be later than usual for Bonny's morning milking but she would suffer no discomfort as a consequence. It was some time since she had calved and, being mostly Highland, she produced a relatively small quantity of milk and therefore was not incommoded by a large distended udder such as that of a dairy cow. I could enjoy my extra hour or two in bed in the morning knowing my charges were provided for. Only Charlie Big Eyes would miss his morning feed and at this stage of his convalescence I reckoned Charlie Big Eyes could very well fend for himself.

I had found Charlie Big Eyes one wild wet morning some three weeks previously hunched dejectedly beside the hen run, his feathers shaggied by wind and rain. When I had thrown a small handful of corn in his direction he had watched with what I thought to be unusually large eyes for a pigeon and when after a moment or two of hesitation he had moved forward to peck at the grain I was able to see that he had rings on both legs. It was not the first time a homing pigeon had honoured me with its presence. Before Charlie Big Eyes there had been Charlie One, then Charlie Two, followed by Charlie Three. Charlie One had arrived in much the same circumstances as Charlie Big Eyes. He too had been squatting dejected and bedraggled by the hen house and since Charlie One was the first 'lost' homing pigeon I had ever encountered I had felt both pleased and flattered that he had chosen my croft on which to seek sanctuary. I threw down some grain and he half-circled it, his gait expressive of both eagerness and caution, but though I spoke coaxingly it was not until I withdrew completely out of sight that he began pecking at the corn with a rhythm that was almost mechanical in its repetitiveness. Initially it was with the intention of restoring him to health and strength so he would be able to find his way back to his rightful home that I regularly fed him grain and mash but as he grew more trusting and his golden eyes came to regard me without suspicion I realized I had grown fond of Charlie One and continued to feed him in the hope that he had forgotten his old home and had now adopted me as his new owner.

Between feeds Charlie One chose to perch on the ridge of the cottage roof and on calm mornings I woke to his anticipatory cooing for food. When the weather buffeted him from the roof he took refuge in the doorway of the byre where he restlessly awaited his morning feed. I knew that he could not survive the really wild weather in such meagre shelter and if he was to remain I had to devise some safe and sheltered place for him to roost at night. The beams of the thatched byre offered a plethora of roosting places to many small birds who poked their way in through the tiny spaces between the walls and the roof, but a pigeon is not a small bird and for Charlie One there was no access to the byre unless the door was left open – and in Bruach a door left open was an invitation to the wind to come in and lift off the roof. Likewise the barn was similarly snug, its drystone walls affording apertures where only wind and rain and mice could penetrate. And again because of the strength of the wind one could not simply rig up a temporary shelter, since even the smallest Bruach structure had to be solid indeed if it was to stand at all. One way out of the difficulty was for Charlie One to share the hen house, but as some of the hens resented his presence and attacked him fiercely on sight it was an impossible solution. The remaining structure on my croft was my own 'wee hoosie', but fond as I was of Charlie One I rebelled at the notion of sharing my privy with a pigeon.

I mentioned the problem of Charlie One's accommodation to Erchy.

'Ach, you'll not need to trouble yourself,' he told me. 'I doubt he'll not be with you much longer.'

I felt a twinge of indignation. 'He's been here for nearly three weeks now,' I pointed out. 'Surely if a bird stays that long he must have adopted it as a new home.' I was careful because of the Bruachites' contempt for sentimentality not to disclose to Erchy that I had already given the pigeon a pet name.

'Indeed you might think that,' Erchy allowed.

'But what I'm sayin' is he'll stay until he's ready to fly away, just.'

I hoped to prove him wrong. Surely, I reasoned, a pigeon's homing instinct would reassert itself as soon as the bird felt fit enough to fly and as to Charlie One's fitness I had no doubts at all. In fact it had taken only a few days of rest and good feeding for Charlie One to recover from his weak, half-starved condition and for nearly two weeks now, sturdy and alert, he had been strutting self-confidently about the croft, his head bobbing perkily; his neck feathers polished to gleaming iridescence by the clean Hebridean rain and wind. Admittedly each day after his recovery he would go missing for a time after his morning feed, but I accepted that birds must fly, and since more often than not when I glanced up at the roof of the cottage Charlie One would be there preening his fluffed-out feathers I was reassured as to his faithfulness. But it continued to distress me that Charlie One had as yet no 'home' where he could be safe from weather and from predators. Casting around for a suitable roosting place which would be within my powers of contrivance, I at last hit upon the idea of making a cavity high up in the peat stack at the end of the cottage. My peat stack was built in the traditional Hebridean way like a buttress against the more sheltered gable of the cottage and I reckoned that if I could remove a section of the stack and then rebuild it with spars of driftwood wedged among the dry peats to discourage them from collapsing, and at the same time provide a perch for Charlie One, I might very well solve the problem. Full of confidence, I set to work the next day, but to build a cavity into a stack composed of brittle odd-shaped peats is no easy task and before long my confidence crumbled as quickly as many of the peats. Even as I stepped back to survey my first attempt the peats collapsed, but with Kiplingesque courage I 'stooped and built again' and yet again and again and the 'worn-out tools' were my hands, which by the end of the day were rasped as if I had been cleaning them on sand-paper. But at last the task was accomplished. Charlie One had his own 'Cosy Cote' complete with perch and droppings board and a 'door' which I could wedge in place at night.

While I had been working I had from time to time thrown grain down, hoping that Charlie One would come and investigate and perhaps absorb the fact that here was a safe roosting place. He had eaten the grain but, as I discovered the next day, he seemed not to have noticed, or not to have accepted, 'Cosy Cote' as a home. The cavity was empty of droppings. Two days later, though he had been present in the morning, Charlie One did not appear for his evening feed, but since he had been absent once or twice before at feeding times and yet had always turned up later I did not worry. However, when he did not appear that evening nor again the following morning I began to feel a mounting dismay; when the next day he was still absent I knew beyond doubt that he had gone. I wondered sadly if he had at last flown off to seek his former home or if he had fallen prey to a buzzard or a hawk or even one of the village cats.

'I've lost my pigeon,' were my first words to

Erchy when I next saw him. I was not aware at the time that there is a Gaelic word which is pronounced very much like 'pigeon' but which translated means 'big fat belly', so perhaps it is not surprising that Erchy, whose first language was Gaelic, should have looked momentarily nonplussed by my announcement. His eyes glinted over me as the right word slotted into his mind.

'Ach, you mean your dove!' he exclaimed. 'Aye, well, did I not warn you it would stay only until it was ready to go?'

I nodded affirmation. 'All the same, I should like to know what's happened to him,' I said. 'Whether he's making back for his own home or whether he's making a meal for a cat or a buzzard.'

'Likely he'll be with the other doves at the cave over there.' Erchy gestured towards the high cliffs that edged the shore. 'That's always where any stray doves end up that I've seen.'

'They go to live with the rock doves?' I was surprised.

'Indeed they do so. An' breed with them, too. There's been that much cross-breedin' with these racin' doves I don't believe there's many of the birds there that are the real wild ones any more.'

As soon as I could I took my binoculars and made my way to the cliffs where, lying in a well-screened cleft of rock near the cave, I was able to watch the comings and goings of the colony of rock doves. It was not long before I spotted Charlie One. His neck feathers glistened with more colours than the neck feathers of the wild birds and of course he was easily identifiable by the rings on his legs, but there was nothing in his behaviour to distinguish him from the rest of the flock with which he appeared to have achieved a happy co-existence. I watched for over an hour, my feelings a strange mixture of discovery and loss. I went home and blocked up the cavity in the peat stack.

Charlie Two stayed with me for only about ten days before he departed but whether he flew home or whether he also joined the rock doves I never knew. Charlie Three had been with me barely a week before a surprisingly apologetic child brought me a tangle of feathers – all that was left of Charlie Three after their cat had finished with him. Charlie Big Eyes had been with me nearly a month, but by now I had grown philosophical about the ways of pigeons. He was welcome to shelter and food if he wished to avail himself of them, but since I accepted that even supposing his homing instinct did not reassert itself strongly enough to lure him away he would in time respond to the call of the wild. Meanwhile I had no intention of again dismantling my peat stack to provide him with a 'Cosy Cote'.

3

'Lovely Bully'

I CONTINUED my search for Bonny while my thoughts ranged over the variety of animals and birds and even insects which I had enjoyed nursing back to health. There was Harry the hedgehog, whom I had found one sharply cold morning of early spring enmeshed in an abandoned piece of fishing net. I thought at first he was dead, but when I put him into a box of hay inside the warm oven he revived slowly but shakily, and after a few hours was well enough to snuffle his way about the kitchen and to lap warm milk from a saucer. I then provided a box for him in a secluded spot beside the haystack to which he returned each day after his nightly foraging. Harry became so tame he no longer raised his prickles when I picked him up and I was sure he would become a permanent resident. I congratulated myself on having acquired a useful pet, but as soon as the weather grew warmer Harry deserted and though the milk I continued to put out each night was always gone by morning I never knew if it was Harry who had drunk it.

Another temporary patient was a sickly baby lamb to which I temporarily acted as 'foster-ewe'. I had been roaming the hills when I found the lamb, which appeared to have been deserted by its mother, and I wondered if perhaps the ewe, having given birth to more than one lamb, and subsequently having been forced to protect her progeny from a marauding hill fox, had forsaken the weaker. Perhaps my coming upon the scene had caused the fox to abandon his prize temporarily, in which case he would no doubt be in hiding near by waiting to return and claim of his victim the moment I was out of sight. Determined to intervene, I carried the lamb to the shepherd's cottage, but there was no one there when I arrived. No one even within hailing distance and I guessed the shepherd must himself be out on the hill while his wife was probably engaged at the 'Big House'. It seemed best that I should take the lamb home and this I did, putting it into the inevitable hay-lined box beside the stove where I tried to feed it warm milk from a spoon. My efforts were totally unsuccessful. The lamb was too feeble to be interested and the milk ran out of its mouth almost as quickly as I spooned it in. It was too long a walk to go back to the shepherd's house, so I hastened to Morag's cottage where I found Erchy and Hector taking a quiet strupak with her in the kitchen. I asked if any of them knew where I might borrow a baby's feeding bottle.

They looked at me askance. 'Indeed, mo ghaoil, but where would you be findin' such a thing hereabouts? Surely a woman that's fit enough to have a bairn is fit enough to feed it herself. That's what we say here.' She spoke with pride. Morag had once boasted to me that Bruach women did not find childbirth painful so it seemed to follow that they were invariably able to feed their babies themselves. I had to admit that I had never seen a Bruach baby being fed from a bottle but I wondered if someone sometime had brought a feeding bottle to Bruach.

'I mind tsere was a tourist here once wiss a baby an' she was after feedin' it from a bottle,' Hector recalled. 'Tse Dear knows why she had to do tsat all tse same when she had breasts on her tsat big you could swear it was two peat creels she had under her blouse, whatever it was she kept inside tsem.'

'Didn't you find out?' interjected Erchy. 'Man, you must be gettin' old.'

Hector slid him a look of disapproval. 'Ach, she was from Glasgow and tsere's women tsere tsats no more use to a bairn tsan a starved cow tsat goes dry after calvin' just. No, nor to a man either.'

'I suppose the shepherd would have teats?' I suggested.

Erchy drew the palm of his hand across his mouth. 'Damty sure his wife has, anyway,' he said, and looked boldly at Hector for confirmation.

'Whisht!' Morag admonished them. 'He might,' she said in reply to my suggestion. 'Though why he would when he has a mouth on him I'd not be knowin'.' Before I could ask what she meant she went on, 'Why do you no ask Janet's brother Hamish to take a look at the beast? Hamish is as good with sheep as the shepherd himself.'

I found Hamish outside his cottage weaving new hazel wands into an old peat creel.

'You're busy!' I gave him the greeting which in Bruach was tantamount to a polite request for him to spare me some of his time.

'Aye, indeed.' He released a brief, yellow-toothed grin. 'Janet's grumblin' she has no bottom to her creel an' she's after losin' the peat out of it,' he explained. 'I was wantin' to finish it tonight just.' Thus he let me know with reciprocal politeness that, though help if I needed it would not be refused, I must remember that he had other work to do. I told him about the sick lamb.

'See an' just go away inside an' have a wee word with Janet,' he instructed me. 'I will be over in a whiley.'

Hamish joined us almost before Janet and I had finished greeting each other and together the three of us set off for my cottage. He inspected the lamb.

'The poor wee thing,' he murmured gently. 'I'm thinkin' it's like to die on you.'

Janet looked at me and then at her brother. 'Can you no' do anythin' for him?' she asked.

'Indeed I cannot say.' The doubt in his tone made it sound as if he was reluctant to be involved in any attempt to succour the lamb.

Janet, whose role in the household was somewhat matriarchal, pinned him with her glance. 'A wee droppy milk,' she suggested compellingly.

'Aye, then,' agreed Hamish.

'Warm?' I asked, hastening to get the milk.

'No, no. Straight from the bowl just if you have it,' he said.

When I had brought the milk Hamish tenderly lifted the feeble little body of the lamb on to his knees and turned its head towards him. 'See now that you watch what I do,' he told me. 'It's what you must do yourself if you're thinkin' to save him.'

I watched interestedly as Hamish took a gulp of milk from the cup and holding it in his mouth for a few seconds slowly shook his head from side to side as if he was using it for a mouthwash. Then he bent forward and lifting the lamb's head he brought his own mouth down on to the open mouth of the lamb when, like a bird regurgitating into the rictus of its young, he allowed the milk to dribble slowly from his mouth into the mouth of the animal as he gently stroked its throat. He took another mouthful of milk and repeated the process of regurgitation. This then was what Morag had been referring to when she had mentioned the shepherd having a mouth. I continued to watch with steadily increasing nausea, mindful that this was merely a demonstration of what I myself was now expected to do. My resolve to save the lamb wilted. Even a healthy baby lamb is not on intimate acquaintance a particularly sweet-smelling object, and this lamb, damp with his own urine and sticky with mucous, was decidedly malodorous.

Hamish put the animal back into its box. 'That will do for him now,' he pronounced, wiping the dribbles of milk off his stubbly chin with the cuff of his jacket. 'See now an' do the same again before you go to bed. I'll be over an' take another look at him in the mornin' supposin' he's still alive.'

Janet noticed my stricken expression. 'Do you think you can do it yourself now, mo ghaoil?' she asked, but the concern in her voice was belied by the impish gleam in her eyes.

'Surely she can,' Hamish asserted for me. 'Indeed there's nothin' to it once you've seen it done. Don't give him too much at a time, that's all.'

Janet continued to regard me with amused commiseration. 'No, but I'm thinkin' Miss Peckwitt's not goin' to enjoy herself doin' it,' she said, and this time she was unable to disguise her enjoyment of the situation.

'No, but you're going to enjoy the thought of my misery,' I countered with a stoical grin.

She laughed outright. 'Ach, mo ghaoil, I'm feelin' that sorry for you I would come an' do it myself but that I promised faithfully I would go over an' ceilidh with old Flora this evenin'.'

We exchanged understanding grins. We both

knew that Janet's faithful promises could be shed as easily as old clothes if she felt so inclined.

'I'll do it,' I told her, and ignored her dubious head-shake.

After they had gone I again inspected the lamb. Already it seemed to me to be fractionally stronger and as I fluffed the hay gently around its body to keep it warm the pathetically faint nicker it gave did much to stiffen my resolve to try to nurse it back to health. All the same, I was glad I had a good hour in which to overcome my squeamishness sufficiently to emulate Hamish's example.

Next morning the lamb was perceptibly stronger, though I hardly dared eat for fear of regurgitating more than warm milk into the animal's gullet. When Hamish came he cautiously predicted that he might be able to get hold of a teat of some kind when there was a possibility of the lamb having recovered enough to suck milk from a bottle. By now of course the story of the orphan lamb was all round the village, and as a result I was not surprised though I was immensely relieved when the following day, Hamish arrived at the cottage triumphantly displaying on the palm of his hand what he referred to as a 'tite', though at first glance it looked to me more like a plug than a teat. He dipped the teat into warm milk before inserting it into the lamb's mouth and I felt discouraged when instead of gripping it eagerly as I had expected the lamb remained unresponsive, refusing to hold the teat in its mouth. With infinite patience Hamish continued coaxing until at last the lamb accepted the teat and began to suck, weakly at first and then with steadily increasing enthusiasm. Gradually my stomach unwound itself from the coil into which it had tightened during the regurgitation period and I was able to look forward once more to the enjoyment of my own food.

'He'll do at that,' said Hamish, after putting the lamb back into the box. 'But if you're wise you'll see an' take him back to the shepherd before he's much older. He's more used to doctorin' young lambs an' supposin' you keep him here you might never get rid of him except to the butcher.'

I nodded firm acceptance of his advice. I had every intention of returning the lamb to the shepherd as soon as it was strong enough to fend for itself. But I knew Hamish was right to remind me that I should not grow too fond of the animal, both for its sake and my own. There is no doubt that a hand-reared lamb can become an unmitigated nuisance once it is fully grown and I recalled how, when I was new to Bruach, I had found a friendly sheep out on the hill and, thinking it was lost, had guided it back to the village, only to be upbraided by the irate owner, who, it transpired, had spent the whole of the previous day walking the animal to the remoter slopes of the hills in an attempt to 'lose' it. That lamb had been hand-reared and had quickly become a pet with the crofter's children, but it had been kept too long as a pet and the outcome had been an unhappy one. Even before it was full-grown the crofter's wife was heard to grumble about its misdeeds. It banged its way into the meal shed, she complained, where not only did it help itself from the open sacks of meal and grain but it spilled as much as it ate, which encouraged the hens to come and join in the feast. On fine days when the door of the cottage was more or less permanently open the lamb went into the kitchen when no one was there, where it had intentionally or unintentionally more than once knocked over pails of milk and stood in setting bowls of cream. On stormy days when the door was firmly shut it was in the habit of planting itself firmly in the doorway ready to butt its way inside the moment it saw its chance and though strong men found it easy enough to eject an unwanted sheep from their path, a woman, encumbered as she so frequently was with a bowl or pail or both, found wrestling against the wind to open the door enough of a hazard without the added menace of attack by a hard-horned, determined and wet-fleeced sheep.

The crofter had tried tethering the sheep, but good grass had to be reserved for hay and poor land was either too stony or too boggy for a stake to hold against the persistent straining of an animal which with the perverseness of its kind was constantly striving to feed beyond the circle of the restraining rope. It was forever breaking free, invading near-by crofts and eventually becoming the cause of so many acrimonious exchanges that there was united insistence on its disposal.

The only alternative to slaughtering was for it to be taken and 'lost' among the flocks of hill sheep and, yielding to the entreaties of his children, this the crofter had attempted to do. My action in 'rescuing' the sheep had, alas, only hastened its journey to the butcher.

Mindful of Hamish's advice and determined not

to become anthropomorphic about my patient, I gave him no pet name save 'Lamb', which only when I forgot my resolves was gentled into 'Lammy'. When he had grown sturdy and taken to following at my heels like a faithful dog I tried to feel no pleasure and when, with the strong encouragement of my neighbours, I felt the time had come for him to join the sheep on the hill I carried out my resolution of returning him unquestioningly to the shepherd. But I confess I hated doing it. One cannot succour any ailing young thing; cradle its little body in one's aproned lap; feel the rhythmic pull of its sucking on the feeding bottle; watch the ecstatic glazing of its eyes as the warm milk reaches its stomach; observe with pride its growth from weakness to frisky strength, and yet still remain completely detached.

'You'll be well rid of him,' the shepherd observed, as he pushed Lammie into a small enclosure with two other lambs which his wife had hand-reared and which were also now due to join the hill flocks.

I turned to the shepherd's wife. 'How do you feel about letting them go after you've reared them?' I asked.

She smiled obliquely. 'When he first brings them home I'm as soft over them as I'd be over a bairn,' she admitted. 'But when they're grown they're just sheep an' I'm the best pleased of everyone when they're back on the hill where they rightly belong.'

I looked at her closely, wondering if she was hiding her true feelings and seeing my serious expression she chuckled. 'Come away in an' we'll have a strupak to celebrate gettin' rid of them,' she said.

I had crossed the strath now and was approaching the spot where Tearlaich had reported seeing Bonny and the bull and pausing beside a tumble of rocks from which an isolated young rowan tree reared itself like a flag, I scanned the moors for a glimpse of them. It was habit now when my wanderings brought me this way to pause beside the young rowan tree. When I had first come to Bruach to spend what was intended to be a month or two's holiday I had on my very first exploration of the moors discovered the rowan tree; a struggling seedling with its roots clamped between two bald boulders where there was no visible trace of soil. Intrigued as to how it was possible for the seed to have germinated let alone grown under such conditions, I began to visit it regularly and observe its development. Foreseeably the rate of growth had been slow and even after more than ten years it was still no more than a slender sapling and no taller than myself. But despite the ferocity of the storms which had already trained the few stunted sallows to permanent obeisance the rowan had grown straight and proud; a slim soldier of a tree battling grimly against the harshness of the seasons; the storms of winter; the spring droughts, and most cruel of all the treacherous summer gales which stripped it prematurely of its foliage and left it looking so wearied by its combat that I wondered how much longer it would be before it succumbed to the mastery of the seasons. There was a single rowan tree on my croft; a tall and sturdy tree which every autumn was briefly caparisoned with rich red berries that the gluttonous starlings had usually harvested before I realized the berries were ripe. I had never seen a berry on the lonely little rowan; only wind-shredded foliage, but it continued to survive and in time it became for me not just a landmark but a symbol of courage and tenacity and I never passed it without sliding my hands caressingly down its slender trunk.

I detected Bonny, with Crumley in close attendance, just outside the boundary fence and in the hope that she might temporarily desert him and come to me I climbed on the gate and holding out the potach in my hand began to call. As soon as she heard my voice she looked up and started a few eager paces towards me, but then, seeing Crumley was not following her, she coyly lowered her head and resumed grazing.

'Bonny!' I called again and again, trying to infuse both cajolery and command into my call, for though by now I was a seasoned enough crofter to accept the presence of a bull on the moors during the summer months I had never quite succeeded in overcoming my fear of bulls, particularly when, as tonight, there was no other human being within screaming distance. My plan was to coax Bonny to come to the gate when I could, with the aid of the potach, persuade her to come through so that I could shut the bull safely on the other side. Once milking was finished all I would have to do would be to let her through the gate where she could rejoin her lover. But tonight Bonny was thrawn. It was uphill to the gate from where she was standing and she was either too tired or too loth to leave Crumley to be persuaded either by my presence or by the offer of the potach. Since I knew the battle of wills could continue for some time, I gave in and, still keeping the fence between us, I walked down the slope towards her. Both Bonny and Crumley watched my approach, Bonny eagerly but Crumley with only moderate interest. However, when I tried to bolster my own courage by scolding Bonny for not coming when I called her his interest increased. I thought he began to look a little menacing and recalled his reputation for being cross. For a few moments I stood chiding myself on my fear and reminding myself that Tearlaich had said the bull would be too 'shagged out' to be aggressive. I tried again to coax Bonny to come closer to the fence with the idea that I might just wriggle through between the wires and, in the case of attack, wriggle quickly back again, and eventually she condescended to detach herself from Crumley and come within about fifty yards of the fence. But she would come no closer. Taking a deep breath and keeping my eyes fixed on the bull, I wriggled cautiously through the barbed wire and moved towards her. Breaking a piece off the potach, I fed it to her and after re-assuring myself that the bull was showing no particular interest in me crouched beside her and started to milk. She began to cud contentedly and, lulled by the fact that Bonny's great belly was now screening me from the bull, the tension within me relaxed a little and resting my head against her warm flank I allowed the worst of my fears to be soothed away by the sound of the milk spurting rhythmically in to the pail. Bonny turned her head towards the spot where she had left Crumley and paused in her cudding to send him a gently loving low.

'All right, old girl,' I comforted her. 'We're nearly finished now so you'll be able to go back to him in a wee while.'

The next moment fear bounced against my stomach like a squash ball as the bull appeared in front of me and I crouched petrified as he moved a pace or two closer. 'It's all right,' I told myself desperately. 'It's Bonny he's after, not you,' but even had I tried to move his proximity had the effect of pinioning my feet to the ground and, as my chest grew tighter, I started to wonder how long my knees would take to unlock sufficiently for flight. I wondered if Crumley showed signs of attacking would Bonny protect me; wondered about the possibility of diving under her belly and making a swift run for the fence. The bull moved closer; trapping me between himself and Bonny, and my terrified gaze fixed itself on his red-rimmed eyes and on the span of his powerful horns, which at their base where they emerged from the fringe of shaggy hair between his ears were as thick as my forearm and yet which at their extremities were tapered to points as thin as the tip of my little finger. As he thrust his great head forward and his thick pink tongue came out and curled over his snout, I felt as if fear would kill me even if the bull didn't. He began to sniff at my coat. Enlightenment shot through my fear. The bull wanted a potach! Having seen or smelled the piece of potach I had given Bonny, he had now come for his share and since he had come as close as he was now without showing a trace of animosity surely he could intend no harm? Apprehension disintegrated and I was almost light-headed with relief as still shaking I took the remaining potach from my pocket and broke off another piece. Not daring to risk what he might interpret as the hostile action of throwing it towards him I held it out on the palm of my hand just as I had done for Bonny. He hesitated for a moment, blowing quick suspicious breaths over the potach, before his tongue came out to take it with almost kitten-like gentleness. It was incredible! Here I was actually hand-feeding a bull when only a minute before I had been so stricken with terror I felt unable to move. Slowly I rose and stood with my hand resting on Bonny's back, completely unafraid now as I watched him savouring his potach. It was good to have rid myself of my fear of bulls, I gloated, and thought how much pleasanter summer milking and nutting expeditions and evening wanderings would be now that I should no longer have to make surreptitious detours so as to avoid meeting the bull. Never again, I told myself, and felt so brave I wondered if I dared reach forward and tickle the bull between his horns. And then Bonny ruined everything! Her love for Crumley, it seemed, did not extend to sharing her potach with him. She was jealous and turning on him she clouted him with her horns before pushing him aside so as to get at the potach in my pocket. But Crumley also knew the potach was there and he lumbered back preparing to do battle for it. I was caught between the two of them and the situation was dangerous, for while their show of sparring was not to be taken seriously I could easily be knocked over and trampled on in the ensuing struggle. First rescuing the milk pail, I sidled round Bonny and made quickly and calmly for the fence. Immediately they broke off their sparring to follow me and as Crumley snorted irritably behind me the chill of fear played up and down my spine like a jet of icy cold water and I could not prevent myself from breaking into a run. Reaching the fence I scrambled heedlessly through the barbed wire and from the safety of the other side began to rage at Bonny.

'You stupid, rotten cow!' I yelled. 'You can just do without the rest of your potach.'

Always, ever since she had first calved, I had made it a habit to give her half a potach before she was milked and the other half when milking was finished and now she looked shocked and puzzled by my seeming neglect and desertion. I felt no compunction. During the brief interlude when I thought I had shed my fear I had experienced the same lilting joy as when I first realized I could swim and that I could ride a bicycle. I had so much wanted not to be afraid of the bull but now the fear was back where it always had been and I guessed it would be with me always.

Feeling the need to recover from the experience, I sat for a while on a cushion of heather and glared sourly at the two animals, who stood regarding me hopefully for a time until Bonny became disillusioned and turning away began to graze sulkily. Crumley lifted his head and bellowed argumentatively before he too began to graze. I continued to sit while the moors spread themselves with the fine gauze of darkness which in a Hebridean spring passes for night, and then, relenting, I threw the remains of the potach towards them before climbing back to the path along which I had come. At the gate I paused to look back to where the dark shapes of Bonny and Crumley were clearly silhouetted against the light of the sea. It seemed that Bonny had forgiven Crumley for she appeared to be licking his neck. I left them to their love-making.

The following day when I saw Morag I asked her about the strange man I had encountered on the moors.

'Ach, it would be yon man from London that's stayin' with Kirsty an' calls himself a playwright,' she explained.

'How interesting,' I said. 'But I haven't seen him around at all. Has he been here long?'

'Around two weeks since,' she told me. 'An' indeed, Miss Peckwitt, but you're lucky you haven't seen the likes of him for Kirsty is after wishin' she'd never set eyes on the man at all.'

'Why ever not?'

'He's a wicked man, so Kirsty tells me.' Her voice sounded quite vehement. 'A really bad man.'

'Wicked?' I echoed. Bruachites were so tolerant it sounded strange to hear of anyone being described as 'wicked'. 'He looked harmless enough.'

'Wasn't it Kirsty herself told me or I wouldn't be believin' it by seein' him just,' said Morag. 'But Kirsty is sayin' he stays inside the house all day, 'peckin' at a writetyper machine like a cock at the corn, an' it's in the evenin's just that he takes a walk to himself.'

'That doesn't sound very wicked,' I pointed out with a smile. 'Inconvenient for Kirsty, no doubt, but hardly wicked.'

'Indeed no, mo ghaoil. But didn't Kirsty take a look at some of his writin' one day while she was cleanin' his bedroom an' the Dear knows but she says she was like to faint with the shock it gave her.' Morag gave me a significant look and tried hard to feign reluctance to continue.

'Why was she so shocked?' I pressed.

Morag did not look at me. 'It was about dirty men an' dirty women, Miss Peckwitt,' she confided in a scathing whisper. 'Dirty such as you an' me an' decent folk the world over wouldn't think of thinkin' never mind writin'.'

'Really!'

'Indeed it was so.' Morag's voice grew more confiding. 'Poor Kirsty there that's never known a man's hand up her skirts in all her life an' she didn't know what to say to herself when she read it. She couldn't tell the meanin' of some of what was written at first till young Annac that's workin' for her explained about them. Then she couldn't believe her own eyes or ears.' Morag's lips were so tightly pursed that I knew I would have to guess at the subject of the writing and I wondered how much of the contents of the play Kirsty had felt inclined to divulge. I wondered too how explicitly descriptive the writing would have to be to so distress a minister-worshipping and rigidly pious spinster like Kirsty. 'It's upset her that much she's not been able to bring herself to even look at his bed since, never mind make it for him, she's after tellin' me,' Morag continued. 'She has to get young Annac to see to it for her. . . .'

'She's not likely to be wanting him to come back next year,' I observed.

'No indeed,' agreed Morag. 'It's a wonder to me the cushions officers haven't been out after him.' I waited for her to elucidate, knowing it would soon come. 'If they're against us makin' ourselves a wee drop of whisky why wouldn't they be against a man for writin' the things he was after writin'? There's more harm in that to my way of thinkin'.'

We sat together staring contemplatively at the startled-looking sea wavelets racing before the fresh breeze; at the clean carved shapes of the islands; at the gently blue sky strewn with clouds that looked as soft and inviting as white fur rugs; at mists lit with rainbows and mountains silvered with sunlight. Morag turned to me. 'You would wonder, mo ghaoil, would you not, what like of man would come to a place like Bruach to write a play about dirty people in London?' she asked.

4

Fisherman Willy

'IT's back to the herrin' for me next week, if I'm spared,' said Willy with a yawn and as much of a stretch as he could manage in the confines of the wooden armchair.

'Is that so?' asked Murdoch.

'Aye,' Willy confirmed. 'I'm away on the bus in

the mornin'.' He screwed himself round to face Johnny, the bus driver, who was sitting pincered between Erchy and Hector on a low wooden stool which might comfortably have accommodated two small children. 'See now an' don't go without me,' he warned.

'You will need to be there in plenty time, then,' Johnny told him. 'Ruari Hamish has lobsters an' crabs to go away an' there's venison to be sent to the laird. They'll keep me back loadin' them so I'll need to be away early to make up the time.' He looked down at the floor as he was speaking so that Willy should not see the twinkle in his eyes. But Willy was not to be fooled. His own eyes, shiny and speckled as black opals, fixed Johnny briefly before he turned away. 'Ach, to hell with you,' he replied affably.

Though he was a native of Bruach, the village saw little of Willy except between seasons when the fishing boat on which he crewed was laid up for overhaul and painting. To all intents and purposes Willy had forsaken Bruach; rejected the culture and traditions of the croft and had become a mainland-based fisherman, worldly and rough-edged. However, when he made his periodic visits home, to placate his elderly parents who still worked and cherished their small croft, he went through the motions of conforming to the faith and dogma imposed on him by his upbringing, but his attitude was too patently cynical, his observations too glibly satirical, to deceive any but those who wished to be deceived or, as in the Bruach idiom, 'those who would not be seein''. Nevertheless Bruach still regarded Willy as a son of the croft and welcomed him accordingly, particularly at the ceilidhs during the long dark winter evenings when, for the crofters, gossip and story-telling and singing were the only means of passing the time. Willy brought not just news of fishing to kindle the memories of the old men who had been fishermen in their youth but mainland news and anecdotes; stories which never reached the newspapers even had the newspapers reached Bruach, and these along with tales of life aboard the fishing boat and of his own and his mates' frequently bawdy escapades in the various fishing ports ensured him an avid audience, recriminative though the reactions to some of his disclosures might be.

It was at a ceilidh we were gathered now: a homespun, lamp-lit ceilidh in Marjac's house where the room was warmed as much by the number of bodies as by the unstinted fire of peats. Outside a gale was blowing; a gale which we had struggled against as we made our various ways to the ceilidh and now, tight-packed in the small room, we were relaxed and glad to be indoors, grateful for the company and the warmth which cocooned us against the wildness of the night.

Willy was described in Bruach as being 'always the good man for a laugh', but his stories were not always about the lighter side of life and his announcement that he was soon to return to the fishing had been tossed into the shocked silence which had followed his horrifying story of a tinker family on the mainland. He could vouch for the truth of the story, Willy assured us, because the tinker woman concerned had been in the same hospital as the wife of one of his fishing mates. In fact he had seen the woman for himself, 'no more than thirty years of age if she was that an' about as white as her bandages an' so thin you'd think she'd snap in two at a touch'. According to Willy, the tinker family had been living along with others of their kind in an encampment some distance outside the town and one night the husband, a habitual drunkard, had returned home and set fire to the tent in which his two young children were sleeping. The children had perished in the fire and the wife, in attempting to rescue them, had been severely burned about the legs and arms. The husband subsequently vanished from the scene and before proper enquiries could be made the rest of the tinker encampment quickly disappeared. 'An' now she has nothin' an' nobody in the wide world to do for her,' Willy told us. 'An' there she was in the ward of the hospital, propped up with pillows with not a soul to visit her an' her shrivelling like a snail that's had salt on it when anybody so much as came near her as if she would be expectin' a blow from them.'

'Ach, the man must have been a monster, surely?' said Ian, amidst several more compassionate exclamations and head-shakings.

'The poor woman!' Morag said feelingly, and spoke for everyone present.

'Aye, indeed,' agreed Willy, who had clearly been touched by the plight of the young tinker woman. 'My mate's wife what I was visitin' at the time was sayin' herself would have gone over to talk to her only for the woman bein' a tink.'

'I believe I would have made myself go to her, all the same,' mused Morag.

'Ach, what would be the use of it?' asked Willy. 'There's not much you can say to a tink.'

His statement was accepted unquestioningly and in the ensuing silence I suspected each one of us was composing a mental image of the tinker woman, injured, bereft and alone in her hospital bed. Willy, reckoning we had been given sufficient time truly to absorb the story, deliberately changed the subject by announcing his imminent departure and there was a perceptible lightening of mood.

'Were you after sayin' one of your mates was marrit then?' asked Morag. 'I thought I minded you sayin' once you were all bachelors aboard your boat except for the skipper.' Morag's memory was like a bulging file.

'I did say that. But one of them got married about a year since an' now there's another got himself engaged or somethin' like it,' said Willy. He gave a short bark of laughter. 'He's no very pleased about it either,' he went on. 'I was ashore with him one weekend an' there was this girl waitin' for him. He'd been havin' it off with her for a whiley an' she wasn't a bad looker either. Anyway, he brought her into the pub an' after he'd had a good drink he goes out the back to open his trousers. When he comes back he's lookin' as vexed as if he's lost his taste for whisky. "What the hell's wrong with you?" I says. "Life's hell, that's what's wrong with me," says he. "I wish I hadn't come ashore. I go to try an' make a telephone call an' the telephone's engaged; I just go out to the lavatory an' that's engaged an' now haven't I got to make an honest woman of this lassie I've been goin' about with so now I'm engaged. I tell you, Willy, life's hell, an' I'll be damn glad to get back to the boat."'

'It's yourself will be gettin' marrit next then,' said Mairi Tonag (Mairi with the broad bottom) when the laughter had subsided. There were renewed titters from some of the young girls but Willy ignored them.

'I might at that,' he admitted. 'I was nearly engaged myself once anyway.'

'You engaged?' Mairi's voice was sharp with mockery. 'Who would be thinkin' of gettin' themselves engaged to you?' she teased. 'I don't believe you would stay with one woman more than a week without she would be waitin' on the quay to grab you every weekend.'

'There's plenty would have me if I gave them the chance,' countered Willy. 'An' this one I was speakin' of was good an' ready to have me.'

'Then she couldn't have had much in the way of looks to her,' Janet said with a wink at Mairi.

'That's not true, then,' Willy refuted. 'She was a lovely girl an' a lot of the fishermen was fallin' over themselves to get her.'

'What did she do to you then?' Morag asked.

'She did nothin' to me,' replied Willy. 'But she used to work at the kipperin'.'

'The kipperin'!' repeated one of the girls. She wrinkled her nose and there was a confirmatory chorus of 'Ughs' from the other girls.

'Aye,' said Willy sadly. 'That was the trouble. Every Friday night for a while I used to meet her for a drink an' then take her to the pictures. She used to smother herself in that scent they call "Californian Poppy" so I wouldn't notice the kipper smell. God! but she made herself smell lovely. Honest! I used to love that scent. But then as soon as the cinema began to warm up there comes the smell of kippers. Ach, I couldn't get away from it. The time would come when I'd be thinkin' of a nice hot cuddle an' there on the film would be a lovely garden maybe with the heroine smellin' at a rose before the hero gives her a nice smackin' kiss, but when I turn to do the same to my girl up would come the smell of kippers. Terrible strong it was.' Willy sighed. 'Aye, she was keen enough on me, right enough, an' she was a lovely girl but I never could bring myself to marry her. All the same, I miss her. Whenever I get the smell of kippers I think of her an' what a nice girl she was.' There was a reminiscent smile on his face.

Mairi Tonag shook her head, and still teasing said, 'I don't believe she would have got to marryin' you all the same. A woman wants a man that will stay with her an' not be goin' away with any woman that takes his fancy.' Willy did not see her wink at us.

'I'm no' the one for that,' he protested indignantly. 'Now if you were speakin' of Thigh Jim that crews on a neighbour's boat I'd agree with you. God! He's a right one, that one.'

'Thigh Jim?' echoed Morag.

'Aye, they call him that because he never takes his thigh boots off if he can help it.'

'Not even to go to his bunk?' asked Morag incredulously.

'Not even in his bunk,' affirmed Willy. 'The only time you'll see Thigh's boots off his feet is when he's got a woman somewhere.'

'He does take them off for that?' queried Johnny with pretended surprise.

'Aye, he's made a habit of that,' agreed Willy. 'Too much of a habit. God! He's a laugh, that one. I mind he was in a bar once an' this tart sneaked him into the ladies' lavatory. After a while the barman got to suspectin' somethin' an' went an' banged on the door, shoutin' to the tart to get rid of the man she had. The tart shouted back swearin' there was no man with her. "Then who the hell does this great stinkin' pair of thigh boots belong to?" asks the barman.' Willy briefly inspected his fingernails which were as thick and ridged as cockle shells before turning on the company with a saucy grin that was the equivalent of a dig in the ribs. 'That's how habit kind of lets you down,' he said, and glanced ironically at the excessively virtuous Kirsty whose eyes were closed almost as tightly as her lips.

'Ach, the man!' said Morag scathingly.

'He would not be an island man, surely,' defended Anna Vic.

'Ach no. He was from the east coast somewhere,' Willy said. 'They come pretty rough from those parts.' It was possible to detect something like a sigh of relief at his assurance that it was no island man.

'I'm wonderin' where you were yourself while he was off with his tart, as you call her,' taunted Johnny. 'Likely you would be off with one of your own.'

'Indeed no, I'm not much of a one for tarts,' Willy denied. 'Though God knows there's plenty around waitin' for us lads when we get ashore, particularly when they've heard we've had a good week. Some of them are as old and ugly as the Devil himself too. I don't know how Thigh can go with them. Honest,' Willy went on, 'there was an old cow tried her best to get hold of me once when I'd a good drink on me. Right enough I was drunk but I wasn't drunk enough to look at her. I would as soon have gone to bed with a beast. "Away with you, woman," I told her. "Your face makes me sick." "You're not so good-lookin' yourself," says she. "Maybe not," says I, "but if I had a face like yours I'd go down an' stand in the Square an' pay the kids a shillin' each to throw shit at it."' Willy's grin broadened at the gasps of remonstrance; the sly grins and the appreciative chuckles with which his story was received. 'She left me alone after that.'

'I should think she would indeed,' gurgled Janet.

'Mind you, she got her own back on me, the bitch,' Willy continued. 'She worked on a couple of Irish blokes that was in the bar to pick a row with me an' we started fightin'. I ended up spendin' the weekend in gaol.'

'Oh, be quiet! You did not, surely?' reproached Janet.

'I did so,' insisted Willy. 'A crumby little gaol it was too. Nothin' but a wooden pillow on the bed they gave me. I had to take off my seaboot socks an' put them under my head before I could get to sleep an' there was I dreamin' all night there was a stinkin' corpse in the cell alongside of me.'

'Did you see the woman again at all?' asked Morag.

'I did not then,' said Willy. 'I didn't go ashore for a week or two an' then we were away with the boat some place else so thank God there was water an' not land between me an' her.'

'I'm thinkin' you deserved whatever you got,' Kirsty told him righteously.

Willy turned and bestowed on her an impenitent grin.

Marjac put down the sock she was knitting and lifted the bubbling kettle from the chain above the fire over to the hob. Picking up the empty teapot, she fondled its shiny brown plumpness for a moment and looked a little vague as if she had forgotten something. We understood so well. This was Bruach's famine period: the hens were having their winter rest from laying; most of the cows had gone completely dry in anticipation of the spring calving and even those which continued to milk yielded only a few squeezings, barely enough to provide milk for the family 'strupaks' and, as if to emphasize the scarcity, the weekly grocery van had disposed of its entire supply of tinned milk before it reached Bruach. 'Milk in winter is like honey to the palate,' the old crofters used to say and anyone who has had to endure winters of milkless tea and coffee and has had to eat porridge or cereal without even a dribble of milk to help it down will fervently agree. We all felt deprived by the shortages but to someone as naturally hospitable as Marjac it must have been truly distressing not to be able to offer her guests a 'wee strupak'.

With a sigh she replaced the teapot on the hob and again took up her knitting. A brief, slightly awkward silence was broken by an outburst of protesting shrieks and giggles, the result of young Uisden having furtively produced a dried 'sea wash ball' (the dried cases of whelk eggs) and scraped it along the back of Catriona's hand. Erchy got up and helped himself to a drink from the water pail; Ian reached for a glowing peat from the fire to relight his pipe; Johnny flicked a cigarette across to Willy, and Ian then turned, proffering the glowing peat as a cigarette lighter. Two of the younger children helped themselves to dry peats from the pile beside the hearth and used them as seats. Outside the wind continued to thump against the walls of the house and roar full-throatedly down the chimney.

Murdoch spat into the fire. 'I'm thinkin' there'll be no much fishin' if this weather gets any coarser,' he observed.

'The Dear, but it's wild, wild, wild,' corroborated Padruig amid a rumbled chorus of assent.

For ten days and nights the gale had been romping through the village, fortunately not with the near-tornado force of the severe storms which, during the next three months, were likely to beset us, but still with strength enough to make outdoor work at least three times more difficult and tiring even for the tougher Bruachites, who almost from the cradle had been learning the skill of combating the wind. This was a boisterous gale rather than a savage one; it had changed direction frequently and had sometimes been accompanied by a mixture of sleet and snow; sometimes by hard-driven rain that was as cold as snow, and sometimes by fusillades of hailstones that ranged from pill to mothball size, and we had now reached the stage of fretfulness when we longed for even a brief respite. But as yet there seemed little prospect of the wind abating.

I tried to imagine what it would be like on the open deck of a fishing boat in such conditions, contending not only with the weather but with the merciless, unpredictable sea, and my gaze rested on Willy's sturdy body, his weather-taughtened face and his hands, broad as wash-basins and with rough, stubby fingers that stayed permanently half clenched as if they could never quite relax their grip on the salt-hardened ropes.

'Ach,' said Willy, dismissing Murdoch's doubts. 'The weather can do what in the hell it likes but it won't make any difference to our skipper. That's a man that's mad for the fishin'.'

'Did you get good fishin' last season?' asked Erchy.

'Good enough,' replied Willy. 'The prices weren't so good though an' a lot went for fish meal.'

I said, 'It seems tragic when good fish is made into meal that's often used for fertilizer when in other countries there are people dying from starvation.'

'It might seem that way,' agreed Willy, turning to me earnestly. 'But you see, Miss Peckwitt, it likely wouldn't do them any good if they got it. I mind our skipper tellin' us about a firm he knew that once dried a lot of the herrin' an' sent it out to one of these foreign places where the folks were supposed to be starvin' to death. An' he said the natives didn't know what to make of it. They thought they'd been sent a load of roofing tiles so they nailed them on the roofs of their huts to keep the rain out. As true as I'm here,' he said, seeing my doubtful smile. 'The firm got word back sayin' they didn't want any more of the same sort.'

Murdoch said, 'Your skipper doesn't mind how much sea there is, then?'

'I'll say he doesn't,' responded Willy. 'An' he'll have us shoot the nets supposin' we tell him they're likely to come up as empty as a hake's belly.'

'As empty as a hake's belly?' I said quickly. 'I've never heard anyone use that expression before. Why do you say that?'

Willy looked surprised at my sudden interest. 'Why wouldn't I say it?' he replied. 'There's nothin' as empty as a hake's belly can be when you catch it.'

'It sounds so strange,' I pointed out. 'Why particularly a hake and no other fish?'

'Because a hake's not like other fish,' he explained. 'I reckon a hake can digest its food quicker than any creature in the sea. The only time we ever get a hake with food in its stomach is when it's been able to eat the fish caught in the net along with it.' Willy looked across at Murdoch as if expecting the old man to contradict him, but Murdoch only nodded.

I sat back, cherishing this new snippet of information and wondering if some day I should be able to confirm Willy's theory in some reference book. I doubted it. Fishermen acquire so much knowledge of the mysteries of life in the sea; strange facts which they accept so easily yet do not bother to disclose so one does not necessarily find what would be called 'expert' confirmation. I lived near the sea; the sound of it was so constant that unless I made myself consciously listen it was inaudible; I watched it, rowed on it, even fished in my small way but I was always aware that relatively speaking I was but an observer. Except by reading and by listening to the talk of men who at some time in their lives had sought and fought the sea for a living, I would never learn more than a fragment of its mystery.

'You must find some pretty strange things in your nets sometimes,' I prompted hopefully.

'I'll say we do,' affirmed Willy. 'Why only last time we were out the skipper was askin' us to put a name to some of the queer beasties we got in the net.'

'What like were they?' asked Murdoch, taking the pipe out of his mouth.

'For all the world like red balloons,' said Willy. 'An' they live in deep water too. On the sea bed.'

'They'd be some kind of starfish or anemones likely,' suggested Erchy.

Willy spurned the suggestion. 'Starfish be damned,' he retorted. 'D'you no think I've been long enough at sea to know a starfish or an anemone when I see one? No, it was neither,' he went on. 'I'm tellin' you when you pick up one of these things it sends out a great squirt of muddy water an' crumples like a burst balloon, yet when we tried cutting one open it had the stomach an' entrails of an animal. We didn't know what to make of them.'

'Indeed I never heard of such things,' exclaimed Janet. 'Surely the sea is full of wonders.'

Padruig Glic (Padruig the wise) asked thoughtfully, 'Did you say they were red?'

'Kind of red,' agreed Willy.

Padruig nodded. 'They would be what the English call a "sea squirt",' he elucidated, and added with an oblique smile, 'The name we have for them in the Gaelic means "a long-drawn-out fart".' Amid wheezes and chokes of laughter everyone looked at me.

'That's just what they do, then,' said Willy with a grin. 'Surely there's no language like the Gaelic for puttin' a right name to a thing.' He aimed his cigarette butt at the fire and rooted in his pocket for the packet. 'If it's strange things we're speakin' of there was somethin' we got only a few weeks back in the net. It was that big an' heavy we couldn't haul the net at all though we tried every which way. The skipper thought he was goin' to have to cut the nets free an' lose them but then all of a sudden up they came as easy as you like.'

'An' what was in it?' asked Johnny eagerly.

'Nothin',' said Willy.

'Nothin'?' repeated Johnny incredulously. 'What do you reckon was keepin' it then, a rock?'

'It was no rock,' returned Willy. 'The way we was haulin' a rock would have torn our net to shreds. When we got the net in we thought it would be damaged but there wasn't a hole in it.' He looked around at the varying expressions which ranged from wide-eyed wonder to carefully concealed scepticism. 'I'm thinkin' it must have been a monster of some kind,' he went on defiantly. 'A monster that was able to swim out of the net when it wanted.'

'Ach, monsters!' broke in Tearlaich with a yawn. 'If you believe everythin' you hear there's a monster in every loch in Scotland. Half the time I'm thinkin' folks are lookin' at a conger eel through a magnifying glass.'

'I don't know about lochs but it's true there's plenty of monsters in the sea,' Willy maintained.

'Damty sure that's true,' supported Erchy.

Tearlaich, who probably had less experience of the sea than any other man present, shrugged contemptuously.

'Mind you,' conceded Willy with a cheerful smile, 'maybe it's not just humans who see monsters. We had a fellow aboard once that wore these thick glasses like the bottoms of glass bottles; we called him "Square Eyes", an' one day when he was helpin' to haul they fell off into the sea. The crew had a great laugh tellin' him they'd landed on the head of a big cod, so there's a panic-stricken cod swimmin' around the Minch thinkin' every sprat is a monster chasin' him.'

'An' what would the poor man do on a fishin' boat without his glasses,' asked Morag, her mind flying immediately to the serious side of the anecdote.

'Ach, he was no use at all,' Willy told her. 'But he wasn't much loss seein' he was goin' off anyway. The skipper paid him off that week.'

'Goin' off?' asked Mairi. 'Where?'

'Off his head,' Willy said. 'He'd got religion pretty bad when he came aboard but when he started sayin' he was Jesus Christ he properly upset the skipper. "If you're Jesus Christ you make sure our nets come up full of fish," he told him, "because if they're not you can start walkin' back to that bloody harbour."'

5

A 'Right Ceilidh'

I FELT it was time to leave the ceilidh, but as I stood up to go there was a sudden frenzy of hailstones which rattled like shot against the window and hammered on the roof. I sat down again.

'Indeed they near deafen the ears off me,' complained Morag when the onslaught had subsided and we could once more make ourselves heard.

'Aye, isn't that just what I'm after sayin',' Murdoch spoke as if he was replying to the storm rather than commenting on Morag's remark. 'I doubt there'll be little enough fishin' supposin' it's for mackerel or monsters if this weather doesn't quieten.'

'It's nothin',' said Willy easily.

'Nothin'?' expostulated Murdoch. 'Man, I tell you I canna put in my teeths when I go out for fear the wind will blow them down my throat every time I open my mouth.'

'You'd best be puttin' a string on them an' tyin' them round your neck then,' suggested Erchy waggishly.

'Ach, it's nothin' I tell you,' reiterated Willy. 'Not to a good boat.'

'She must be a good strong boat you have,' said Erchy.

'Aye,' Willy's voice verged on the reverential, 'She's a good boat right enough.'

The knowledge and love of boats is instinctive in most islanders and the talk soon drifted to the merits and de-merits of boats the Bruachites knew or had known. Boats which had been wrecked; boats which had been bought or sold or laid up because they could neither be crewed or sold. And it was not only the men who indulged in the discussion and recollection. The women too participated, though, as might be expected, their observations were more concerned with the genealogies of the owners and crew rather than with the boats themselves. As when, for instance, the widow Hamish interpolated: 'I mind that man when he was a bairn and if ever there was a wee monster it was that one.' Or again Morag's interruption of an argument as to the qualities of a certain skipper with the question: 'Was he not yon man who had the wife that was condensed from Church of Scotland into a Roman Catholic?'

As I listened I found myself mentally attaching faces and shapes to the names of people as I heard them mentioned; people I had never known and would be unlikely ever to meet; people who in truth most of the Bruachites had never known except by allusion and who they were equally unlikely to meet, though, as was their custom, they had elevated such proxy acquaintance into a much more personal relationship. The ceilidh voices rippled on; old and young intermingling; some softened by memories, some sharpened by argument. I glanced covertly about me. In too many Hebridean villages the tourist invasion combined with increasing mobility had virtually put an end to ceilidhing as we in Bruach knew it, and not for the first time I wished I had the artistic skill to preserve the scene as I saw it now. The small room with its low wood ceiling and walls stained harness-brown with years of peat smoke, lamp smoke and tobacco smoke; the small curtainless window set square and black against the night; the gay linoleum, or wax cloth as it was known to the crofters, recently laid with pride but already moulded to the rugged contours of the driftwood floor it concealed; the sturdy wooden table, normally in the centre of the room but now pushed back against the wall to accommodate the company; the squat, so solidly constructed water bench on which reposed two full pails of water with the dipper handy beside them; the capacious oatmeal and flour barrels, each holding at least a hundred and forty pounds of meal, standing side by side in a corner of the room and disguised by fancy wallpaper; the salt barrel holding a minimum of two hundredweights of coarse salt which stood in the opposite corner; the peat bucket beside the fireplace piled to toppling height with neatly shaped peats which were the result of Ian's expert cutting. Clinging to the wall at the right of the fireplace was as almost skeletal clock which, according to Marjac, had stopped so prophetically at eleven o'clock on the first Armistice Day after the Great War that no one had since dared to interfere with it. The painted dresser was chock-a-block with everyday utensils and also was the site for the brass-based oil lamp, with its pink glass bow, glamorizing the paraffin it held and its well-polished chimney already smudged by the draught-tormented flame. There was no rug on the floor; the fender was a stout spar of driftwood and the low black grate it guarded was recessed so far into the thick walls it looked as if it was cowering away from the company and resentful that even a fraction of its heat should escape even temporarily into the room before being sucked greedily up the chimney.

But it was not just the setting that was worthy of portrayal. At the ceilidhs, unless one was wearing oilskins, there was no polite suggestion that one should divest oneself of one's outdoor clothes and certainly in winter few crofters' kitchens would have tempted one to do so. We stayed in our coats and jackets and gumboots; the old men still capped, the old women still bonneted, and we sat wherever we could find space. The old men had appropriated the bench below the window while the old women huddled together on the opposite bench like pigeons on a winter bough. The favoured, such as myself, were given chairs; the middle-aged and the youthful perched on stools and barrels, while the children who were present were perfectly content to sit on a couple of dry peats or simply on the floor.

As always it was the old people who dominated the conversation and it was a delight to watch their composed expressions becoming animated as they winnowed their stored memories; the children appeared to be listening attentively; the youthful were only partly successful in feigning indifference and the rest, like the incorrigible Erchy and Johnny, Hector and Tearlaich, while allowing their habitually firm mouths to relax into half smiles, were always ready with some teasing interjection which they hoped would spark off the spirited argument and light-hearted disputation without which no Bruach ceilidh was complete.

I heard Padruig say, 'She's not a young boat then?' and I realized that the conversation having drifted meantime over a whole fleet of fishing boats and their crews had now returned to the subject of Willy's boat.

'No, but old as she is she's stronger than plenty half her age,' Willy said staunchly. 'The skipper was speakin' of gettin' a new engine in her an' if he was to do that she'd be as good as many a new boat that's sailin' the sea today.'

'That's true enough,' declared Murdoch.

'Was the engine givin' trouble then?' asked Padruig.

'Not what you'd say was trouble,' Willy admitted cautiously, 'but the way the fishin' is goin' these days we could do with more power than we have. Right enough, I believe it would be a good thing to put in a bigger engine.'

'You would be better to get a new boat, maybe,' suggested Johnny.

'Aye, an' then you could have it blessed like them fellows from Uist that had their pictures in the paper. I'm damty sure you'd get good fishin' then,' proposed Erchy with sly daring. All eyes swung towards Kirsty, for though Bruach itself suffered no 'dom papists and their customs' Kirsty was easily the most bigoted. She primmed her thin mouth into an even tighter line but otherwise gave no indication she had heard.

'Indeed if you told that to our skipper I believe he would give you a blow for it,' said Willy. 'To his way of thinkin' you don't ever bless engines, you only curse them; he says that's the only way to keep them running. His wife takes him along with her to church on Sundays but he won't have a minister of any sort near his boat.'

'An' he's right,' endorsed Erchy. 'Ministers and engines don't agree an' it's myself has proved that more than once.'

'I wouldn't have any of tsem buggers blessin' a boat,' Hector derided. 'I was on one of tsese blessin' boats myself for a wee whiley an' it was a wee whiley too long. She was after puttin' me in hospital.'

'In hospital?' echoed Janet.

'Aye,' said Hector. 'Didn't I slip from the mast and land astride a beam across the hold.'

There were shrieks of female laughter and the ever-calfish Elspeth tried to conceal her mirth by biting at her left shoulder as Hector clasped his hands descriptively between his legs. 'God but if it was blessin' tsat boat wanted she got it tsen from me.'

'It must have been serious if it put you in hospital,' said Murdoch sympathetically.

'Serious? Surely it was serious!' said Hector. 'Didn't it worry tse life out of me for fear tse lassies would no' be wantin' anytsin' to do wiss me again?' His glance challenged the girls.

Marjac returned his look. 'Well, it didn't quench your ball of fire,' she assured him brazenly.

'No, tsank God! But I was lucky all tse same,' Hector rejoined. 'Tse nurses all told me tsat.'

'Oh, and what a good time you must have had with all those young nurses attending to you in hospital,' taunted Janet, digging her elbow slyly into Marjac.

'I did not tsen,' refuted Hector, amid exclamations of mocking disbelief.

'I tell you I did not,' he repeated. 'It wasn't tse way you're tsinkin' at all. I was after comin' round from tsis painkiller tsey'd given me an' feelin' all nice and drowsy when tsis hand comes under tse sheet and takes hold of my wrist oh, so nice and gentle like, an' here's me tsinkin' what a lovely sight is goin' to meet my eyes when I open tsem. I couldn't seem to stop myself smilin' at tse tsought. Tsen when I did open my eyes what do I see on tse sheet holdin' my wrist but a great, brawny, tattoed arm tsat was as hairy as a goat. It was horrible. True as I'm here. I'm tellin' you I was so sick I nearly bit it.'

There were peals of delighted laughter and Marjac had to wipe the tears from her eyes with the sock she was knitting.

'An' tse voice of him,' went on Hector, 'Dear God! But it was so bad I told him he should give it a good skelpin'.'

'A male nurse?' murmured Johnny. 'No wonder you got a shock when you saw him. I was forgettin' there were such things.'

'Ach tsey was all male nurses in tsat ward,' complained Hector. 'I never saw a woman except for a cleaner an' she was English. Tse bloody hospital was worse tsan tse accident.'

The wind seemed to be strengthening if anything and a flash of lightning cut across the window. I began to button up my coat again and pulled on my gloves as an indication that I was ready to leave.

'You'll no be goin' yet, surely,' said Marjac with polite remonstrance. 'It's only at the back of midnight just.'

'It's late enough for me,' I replied, rather regretfully. 'Anyway, the weather seems to be worsening and I'd like to try to get home before the next squall comes.'

Morag too stood up, 'I'll be coming with you,' she said.

'Oh, don't!' I protested, thinking she was deserting the ceilidh simply so I should not have to walk home alone. 'I'm perfectly happy to go by myself,' I insisted.

'It's no' that,' said Morag. 'It's just that I'm feelin' myself tired, though the Dear knows why I should be.'

Janet also began to pull her coat round her and belt it with a length of rope.

'Ach, but this is terrible,' Marjac reproached her. 'Whatever is takin' you away at this hour?'

But before she could reply Willy also stood up.

'An' if I'm to get away on the bus in the mornin' then I'd best get home myself,' he said.

Marjac looked so disappointed I felt guilty at having been the first to make a move, though I knew Bruachites did not leave a ceilidh unless they wished to. 'Oidhche mhath!' we called, and quickly opening and closing the door we dashed outside into the full thrust of the gale.

'Oh, my, but it's coarse,' gasped Morag as she stumbled against me.

Not even trying to converse, we pushed against the wind, one hand holding our coats tightly around our bodies while the other held scarves or collars snugly up to our chins. I could feel my cheeks pulling tighter and tighter with the cold and as I looked up at the sky where the last squall could be seen disgorging itself over the hills, the full moon which emerged sporadically from behind throngs of racing dark clouds looked as harassed as if it was trying to apologize for the execrable weather.

'It won't be so bad when we've topped the hill,' panted Janet. 'We should have the wind at our backs then.' But even in the lee of the hill the wind was only a little less tyrannical and already over the sea another squall was fast approaching, looming blackly against the palely lit water. A few intermittent hailstones sent us hurrying to reach the shelter of one of the shallow rock caves beside the road. The caves were known as 'Slochlachans' after Lachlan, a one-time Bruach roadman, who was reputed to have hewn them out of the cliff so as to provide himself with handy refuges where he might rest and smoke a pipe in the intervals between working on the long length of the sinuous Bruach road.

Janet and Morag and I crouched close together and back as far as we could against the rock wall, but Willy, spurning such womanishness, stood protectively in front of us, hunching his back to the wind. We heard the hailstones begin to hurry against his oilskins like an introductory drumbeat rolling to a crescendo. And then it came: the full force of storm-driven, hurtling, hissing hailstones, blotting out land and sea and sky with a harsh impenetrable black curtain. But even as we watched, wide-eyed in the blackness, the curtain was suddenly rent by a double flash of lightning and for the time it took me to gasp I could see the hailstones pouring from the sky in swirling, graceful, silver columns before they were once more engulfed by darkness. And then almost as swift as had been its onslaught the squall ceased, leaving us in a cloistered silence which was accentuated by the distant roar of the sea.

'What else will the sky be after throwing at us tonight?' said Willy, shrugging and beating the hailstones off his oilskin.

Janet looked up at the scudding clouds. 'That's it over for a whiley,' she announced. 'We'll maybe get back before the next one is on us if we're sharp.'

'I do believe they're gettin' further apart,' said Morag. 'Maybe tomorrow will see the end of this storm.'

'We'll be lucky,' said Willy without optimism.

As our feet crunched and skidded on the crisp carpet of hailstones, I was silent, remembering the brief and secret splendour of the storm which the lightning had revealed, but my companions, taking advantage of the lull in the wind, began immediately to converse.

Morag said, 'You mind Willy you was speakin' of yon fellow that was on your boat an' got religion?'

'Square Eyes you mean? The one with the thick spectacles? Aye, I mind him well enough,' Willy replied.

'You didn't say what became of him,' said Morag, to whom an uncompleted story was as pestering as a ragged fingernail.

'He went to a home, that's all that happened to him,' Willy told her.

'An' is he himself again now?' asked Morag solicitously.

'How would I be knowin'?' retorted Willy. 'I didn't keep in touch with the man. All I know is what his brother was after tellin' me about takin' Square Eyes to the home.'

'What did they do with him there?' pursued Janet.

'Well, seemingly this doctor took a look at Square Eyes and then he had a word with the brother.

'We've put him in the Jesus Christ room,' he tells him. 'He'll be all right there for a while.'

'The Jesus Christ room?' Morag sounded appalled. 'How would they have such a place?'

'That's just what the brother was thinkin', said Willy. '"D'you mean to say there's others after goin' the same way?" he asks the doctor. "Aye," says the doctor, "there's four of them there already." "Good God!" says the brother. "What happens when you put them all together in the same room then?" "Ach," the doctor tells him, "by the time they've finished trying to convince one another they're all bloody atheists anyway."'

6

Infernal Gulliver

THE rainwater tank was full to overflowing and the drowned moth lay on the surface of the water, pitifully dead, its outspread wings semi-transparent as if they had already begun to disintegrate. I paused, captivated by the beauty and fragility of the insect, and, dipping a finger gently under it, lifted it out so as to examine more closely the intricacy of its wing pattern. It adhered damply to my finger, totally inert, and yet after only a moment I sensed the faintest tremor of life, so vague that I was not sure at first whether the tremor emanated from the moth or from my own skin. With a kind of doubting surprise I held out my hand, letting the warm sun shine directly on to it and though there was not the smallest movement discernible to my eye again there passed between the moth and my finger a perceptible thrilling of life. I watched intently, still trying to detect some movement and at length was rewarded by a tiny quivering of the wings; a sporadic quivering which grew momently into a tentative fluttering though the moth was still anchored to my finger by its wet body. As the moth gained strength, I felt as if I was witnessing a small miracle of resurrection and I was aware of a feeling of elation. Had new life been imparted to the moth through some emanation from my finger, I wondered, or had it not been truly dead and so had needed only the warmth of the sun to give it a resurgence of life? If the latter then why is it that a cow or sheep, even a human, can so hastily relinquish the will to challenge death on its approach while this tiny insect, which must have struggled for many hours since it was a creature of the night and it was now well into the afternoon, should show such resistance? Can an ephemera like a moth have a stronger sense of survival than a cow? I wondered.

My musings were interrupted by a voice. 'See what I've found!' announced Ian Beag. Putting down a rusted tinker-made pail and a heavy but much-cherished hazel fishing rod he slid a cautious hand up under his flannel shirt and produced a fluffy, moist, grey and black gull chick which looked so new and dazed if Ian had said he had just hatched it rather than found it I would have had no great difficulty in believing him.

'Ian!' I exclaimed, my reaction fading from pleasure to reproval as I caught sight of the slimy smears the chick had left on Ian's bare stomach. Hastily he pulled down his shirt.

'I wasn't wantin' him to get cold,' he explained.

On such a tranquil almost sultry warm day I doubted if there was any danger of that, and Ian, who had clearly been indulging in a far more strenuous activity than fishing, was flushed and shining with sweat. The gull chick too appeared to be feeling the heat. Its beak was gaping and when I took it in my hand its fluff felt damp. Since I doubted if birds could sweat so copiously, I surmised that much of the dampness was due to the chick having been confined for some time between Ian's stomach and his thick flannel shirt. The rest of the dampness was explained by the smell. The gull began to cheep.

'He's nice,' enthused Ian tenderly.

'He's lovely,' I agreed. 'But how did you come to find him?' I strongly disapproved of chicks being taken from their nests and though I was reasonably certain Ian would be party to no such barbarism I wanted to make certain.

'Aye, well, see when I'd done fishin' I went over to Cairn Mhor to try would I get some gulls' eggs an' it wasn't until I was back at the shore that I found this little fellow, I'm thinkin' he was after fallin' from the nest.'

The collecting of gulls' eggs in spring was a regular and much anticipated ploy for the more intrepid of the Bruachites, the eggs providing welcome relief from the monotony of a winter diet of salt herring and potatoes. It sounds a reprehensible practice but there is no doubt that isolation and the consequent frustrations of shopping do much to help one overcome one's scruples as to the source of one's food, so even I who had always regarded the plundering of birds' nests as execrable had soon ceased to be concerned at the annual toll of gulls' eggs.

'You'll have no need to worry,' the Bruachites assured me when I had expressed my concern. . . . 'We take only the infertile just.' Since the Bruach population of gulls appeared in no way to diminish I felt justified in accepting their comforting assurance even to the extent of enjoying the occasional gull's egg omelette.

I pursued my questioning of Ian. 'Are you sure there were no adult gulls near which might have been its parents?' I probed.

'Not a one save a blackback or two.' Ian's eyes, soft and brown as dripping jelly, regarded me with complete candour. 'He was a good way from any nest we could see so I'd say the old birds had given up lookin' for him.' Ian put out a grubby finger and touched the chick. 'Right enough I believe the blackbacks would have got him if I hadn't found him first.'

The fate of a chick at the mercy of a blackback

was too horrible to think about. 'He appears to be a lucky little chick, then,' I said.

'Indeed he is so.' Ian pulled a handful of grass and lifting up his shirt, rather belatedly wiped the smears of gull mute off his stomach, and as an afterthought from the inside of his shirt. 'The cailleach's not goin' to thank me for it when she comes to washin' my shirt,' he admitted with a rueful grin. In Bruach it was not disrespectful for a boy to refer to his mother as the 'cailleach', the literal translation of which is 'old woman'. Indeed to me it sounded rather more affectionate than the alternative 'Maa', the Bruach rendering of which was like the bleat of a hoarse sheep.

I asked one or two more relevant questions before holding out the chick for Ian to take from me. 'Thank you for letting me see him,' I said.

'Ach, you can keep him,' he told me with lofty generosity and before I could demur he continued, 'Seein' the school doesn't take its holiday for a whiley yet I wouldn't be able to look after him anyway.'

Momentarily at a loss, I continued to regard the chick as it sat cheeping in my hand. In Bruach there were gulls everywhere; their crics accompanied the earliest dawn and died only after a lingering dusk. They patterned the sea and the sky and drifted like white feathers against the dark background of the hills. Unlike inland gulls, however, they remained mostly wild and aloof. A few of the less timid ones tended to range in the vicinity of the crofts to forage for hen food, but the main flocks limited their territory to the sea and the hills and even in savage weather sought no closer sanctuary than the distant moors. The nearest I had previously come to familiarity with a seagull had been when a lesser blackbacked gull had taken it upon himself to police my hen run. Why he came and why he eventually deserted his self-imposed guardianship I do not know, but for the best part of the year he had hovered around the hen run at feeding times, and though he stole as much of the hen food as he wanted during the whole of that time he allowed no other gull nor even a hoody crow to intrude upon what he considered his domain. Apart from this my experience of gulls was limited to observation and the discouraging of their presence near the hen run, and certainly I had no desire to embark on the rearing of a gull chick to adulthood. Seeing my lack of enthusiasm, Ian rooted in his trouser pocket and offered me what was presumably his day's catch of four tiny brown trout.

'I was thinkin' maybe you would like these,' he said with an ingratiating smile. 'If you would be doin' without them yourself they would be fine for feedin' the chick likely.' Watching him wiping the fish on his shirt sleeve to clean them of the debris of his pocket, I knew I could easily be doing without them. It was by no means the first time I had been confronted with a gift of burn trout, for though the children of Bruach loved to snatch an hour or two from their allotted chores to go fishing, the fish they caught were considered by their mothers to be too small to be worth cooking and they were returned to the burn or, as occasionally happened, they were bestowed on me, partly I suspect because of the belief which seemed to have gained a hold in Bruach that because I ate such things as wild mushrooms and watercress I was cranky enough to eat almost anything. Admittedly the first time I had been presented with an over-warm handful of flabby, much-fondled trout I had managed to feign a degree of pleasure and, resolutely overlooking their sad state, had cooked and eaten them, but the small amount of flesh I had been able to glean from the bones was so strongly impregnated with the flavour of peat and mud that subsequent gifts of brown trout were surreptitiously mixed in with the hens' mash.

As soon as it saw the fish in Ian's hand the chick became restless and its cheeping grew more urgent. Ian took out a pocket knife and hacking the smallest trout into three pieces offered the first of the pieces to the chick. It swallowed it instantly and immediately cheeped for more.

'Goodness! He must be hungry!' I exclaimed. 'And he doesn't need any coaxing to eat, does he?'

'Not him!' agreed Ian. 'An' you'll see after the first few days he'll be the same with near anythin' you offer him. Whelks an' limpets; bread or potach, even rats an' mice if you chop them up for him first.'

'Ian!' I wailed protestingly.

He flashed me an impish smile. 'He will so,' he declared, 'an' he'll grow well on them, surely.' It was evident he had already convinced himself that I was going to undertake the rearing of the gull chick but I was still hesitant. I had once reared a baby guillemot* which had become so used to

* See *Beautiful just!*

human company that it refused to return to the sea and, as a consequence, had had only a short life. I had been told that gulls develop no such human fixation but I was still reluctant to take the risk.

'I'll bring you limpets an' fish myself when I get the chance,' Ian bribed. I could see he was becoming anxious. Rapidly I assessed the problems I might be faced with; the mess; the necessity of frequent feeding; a place to keep him; but I shrugged them away. After all if I could act as 'foster ewe' to a lamb I ought to be able to become 'foster gull' to a chick.

'Very well,' I said resignedly. 'But I'll need some food for him tomorrow. The way he's eating these trout they aren't going to last him for long.'

'Tomorrow's the Sabbath,' Ian reminded me solemnly.

'Oh, so it is,' I replied with matching solemnity. The Bruach Sabbath was so stiflingly restrictive that even a boy of Ian's age could not be permitted on that day to engage in an occupation as frivolous as picking limpets off rocks. I knew if I needed fish for the chick I would have to seek for it myself.

We fed the chick trout until he seemed replete.

'They'll eat more than their own weight in food at one meal just,' Ian told me. 'Once we weighed an adult gull an' then we fed him all he would eat. When we weighed him again he was near three times as heavy as he was before.'

'And I'm expected to provide for an appetite like that?' I taxed him.

'I'm only sayin' they will,' he replied. 'I'm no sayin' they have the need of it.'

I put the chick down on the sun-warm grass and left him dozing contentedly while I went indoors to find a suitable box in which to keep him. Ian followed me.

'The Dear but I'm as hot as a kettle,' he said, politely helping himself to a drink of water from the pail.

'I'd noticed that,' I said. 'You didn't get as hot as that sitting by the burn fishing.'

'No indeed, but didn't I go gull nestin'?' he reminded me.

'You prefer gull nesting to fishing?'

'No, but when Uishden an' some of the lads came by an' said they'd found out the laird an' a party of his friends was meanin' to go to the Cairn gull nestin' this evenin' we all rushed off to make sure we would get there before him.'

I looked at him quizzically. 'Why do some people begrudge the laird getting some free food for himself?' I asked.

'Ach, it's no' that at all,' Ian hastened to deny. 'It's the way he an' his friends go about it we don't like. See, when we go we take with us a pail of sea water an' we test them as we take them out of the nest to see do they float or sink. If they float we know there's chicks in them so we put them back into the nest an' the gull knows no difference. The way the laird an' his friends does it is to take home every egg he can get hold of an' then throw away any he finds with chicks in them.' Ian paused and then added: 'Ach, he's English so I don't suppose he knows any better.'

I handed him a slice of cake, most of which he crammed into his mouth at the first bite.

'You rival a seagull at gulping your food,' I accused him as I punched a hoarded cardboard box back into something resembling its original shape.

'I would indeed,' he acknowledged, not without a tinge of pride. 'But once my food is down it stays down, you can be sure of that. You cannot be so sure with a gull. Supposin' they're full of food as can be an' yet if there comes a chance of somethin' they're likin' better they'll bring up everythin' that's in their stomachs just to make room for it.'

I looked at him with assumed dismay. 'That's comforting, I must say. That means I shall have to watch both ends.'

Ian turned to me with an expression of sheer delight on his face, which might just as easily have been provoked by my statement as by the offer of a second slice of cake.

'You will need to be puttin' some hay in the box,' he instructed, and accompanied me to the barn where I pulled a few handfuls of hay with which, under his supervision, I made the cardboard box into a cosy nest. 'I'd best be away now,' he said, having apparently satisfied himself that I was capable of coping with the gull. 'I'm after promisin' the cailleach I would go up to the Post Office for her this evening yet.'

'You're already too late for the Post Office,' I warned him. 'You'll have Nelly Elly girning at you for keeping her back from the milking.'

'Ach, I'll give her a couple of gulls' eggs to quieten her,' he replied. 'She's that fond of them I believe she would rise from her bed at midnight to give me a stamp if she saw them.' He indicated the rusty pail. 'Would you like one for your own tea?'

I was on the point of accepting when I remembered I had some sooyan which Erchy had brought that morning, and since they would not keep more than a day I declined the offer of the gull's egg.

Ian picked up his fishing rod and pail and started off down the road.

'Remember your promise to bring me fish,' I called after him.

'I will so, maybe on Monday,' he called back, adding a pious afterthought which sounded strange from one so young, 'If the Lord spares me.'

By this time the chick had recommenced its cheeping. 'All right, Gulliver,' I said, and gave him another feed of trout, after which I lifted him into his hay-lined box where I left him content as I went about my chores. But Gulliver was not content for long. It seemed to me that the more he was fed the more he demanded and after my own evening meal I fed him again, by which time he had consumed all the trout Ian had left and judging from the smell of his box had muted most of it. I re-lined the box with fresh hay and when evening came, indicating its arrival only by a coolness and not by a diminishing of the light, I brought the box indoors, fearing that without the close canopy of a parent gull's feathers the chick would feel the cold. Before I went to bed and in the hope of keeping Gulliver satisfied until the morning, I cut strips from one of the sooyan set aside for my next meal and fed him until he could quite literally eat no more and he began to sway with sleep or satiety while the tail end of a fish was still plainly visible protruding from his gullet.

The days of a Hebridean May are 'as long as today and tomorrow' and with darkness so brief it is hardly more than a gesture. My strategy failed. It was in the small hours of the morning that Gulliver woke me with his unremitting cheepings. I stayed in my bed, my thoughts alternating between drowsy regret that I had agreed to foster the chick and a sense of guilt because I did not rise immediately to attend to him. At the same time I could not help reflecting that such vociferous cheepings surely could not emanate from a bird that was in any danger of dying from starvation and it was therefore safe to ignore him for a while and go back to sleep. I tried to shut my ears but the cheepings bored on into my senses as tormentingly as a dentist's drill and the moment I thought I detected a fainter note I jumped out of bed and, full of remorse, rushed into the kitchen where I was met first by the revolting smell of fish guts and then by Gulliver himself who had managed to clamber out of his box. The evidence of his subsequent wanderings trailed itself over the kitchen floor. I fed him sooyan until he was quiet and back again in his box, then going over to the byre found a piece of old herring net which, when tied over the top of his box, effectively imprisoned him. That done I washed the floor and returned to bed to sleep and to dream disordered dreams which were penetrated by incessant, pestering cheeping. When I woke at my usual time the smell of gull mute permeated the whole house. I rushed to get both Gulliver and his box out into the open air and there he stayed for the rest of the day while the doors and windows of my cottage remained wide open to the deodorizing action of the breeze.

During the day I attended with ever-increasing frequency to the despotic demands of Gulliver, who ate prodigiously, only interspersing his feeds, or so it seemed to me, with minutes of contented repose and hours of agitated protestation that he was hungry. By evening he had disposed of most of the sooyan I had left. By bedtime when I had again carried his box into the kitchen for the night, I had cause to be sorry I had been so generous in the provision of food for after about half an hour in Gulliver's malodorous company I knew beyond doubt that continued cohabitation would be unendurable. I banished him thereafter to the cow byre – unused during the summer months since Bonny was out on the hill – and after cutting down one side of his box to enable him to go in and out at will I shed even more of my responsibility by leaving a plate of chopped fish from which, I reasoned, he could help himself and so survive the night while I slept soundly in my bed.

Gulliver grew incredibly quickly and as each day came I could see a change in him. Fortunately he was soon able to take almost any food that was available. Fortunately because, as I had suspected, Ian Beag, finding more interesting ways of filling his time, soon defected on his promise to supply me with fish and it was I who had to go down to the shore to pick winkles and prize limpets from the rocks. I who had to smash them and pick out the flesh. There were times, as when a storm was accompanied by a high tide, when I could not even do this and I found myself hard put to it to provide suitable food for the chick, though I am glad to say I was never desperate enough to resort to catching and chopping up rats and mice and adding those to his menu as Ian had suggested.

Gulliver's fluffiness was quickly mantled with mottled brown feathers, his voice developed from its importunate cheeping into a less constant but equally importunate thin scream and he took to following me about the croft in the unflagging anticipation of being fed. When, later in the summer, the sea was 'boiling' with mackerel shoals and one could haul in ten fish in as many minutes he would take a whole mackerel in his beak, and it was indeed a comical sight to see him standing with the fish sticking out inches either side of his gaping beak while, without dropping it, he slowly worked the fish back into his gullet until it had completely disappeared, after which he would remain so still it was as if he had stunned himself with his own greed.

When he was fully fledged though still not old enough to have attained the handsome grey and white plumage of a mature gull, I expected that Gulliver would soon be leaving me, but though he often flapped his wings while jumping up and down he was slow in gaining further prowess at flying.

'He's too heavy, that's what's wrong with him,' Erchy told me. 'You've fed him so well he'll not be able to fly.' I suspected he was teasing. 'No, it's as true as I'm here,' he asserted. 'You can see for yourself he's twice as big as any of the other gulls of the same age.' I acknowledged proudly that Gulliver was indeed a fine specimen of a bird. 'Aye, well,' Erchy went on, 'you'll notice even the wild gulls themselves don't take near as much food for a whiley before they start to fly so as to make themselves lighter.' I had noticed nothing of the sort but Erchy was so observant of the ways of wild creatures that I took his advice and experimented by cutting down the number of feeds. It transpired that it was good advice, for not only did Gulliver accept the limitation without complaint but after a few days on a restricted diet he succeeded, with much joyous screaming, in flying up to the roof of the cottage.

Once he could fly Gulliver became playful and his play doubtless being wholly instinctive was interesting to observe. Picking up a small twig he would fly up to about twenty feet, drop the twig and immediately swoop down and seize it again, accompanying this performance with squeaks of delight and repeating it until something else attracted his attention. Sometimes it was a small peeble with which he played in a similar way. At one time I noticed my clothes pegs were disappearing from the box beside the clothes-line post and reappearing, if they reappeared at all, at varying distances from the house. On one occasion when, because both my hands were occupied pegging out the washing I was holding a clothes peg in my mouth, Gulliver landed on my head and swiftly snatched the peg away. When I weeded potatoes he liked to fly down and with a sudden and disconcerting squawk land on my bent back, steadying himself by taking my ear in his beak, or as I was feeding the hens he would land on my head, scrabbling with his webbed feet for a foothold. But there came a time when Gulliver's playfulness developed into something suspiciously like mischievousness.

Dorothy, a friend of my schooldays, and her husband, a retired and rather crustily old-school-type colonel, came to spend a holiday with me. On the day after their arrival, the morning being gilded with September sunlight, they strolled across the croft to watch while I spread small 'prapachs' of hay to dry ready to be built into larger cocks later in the evening. Gulliver had now reached the age when he was able to find much of his own food and after taking his breakfast from me and following it with a ruminative hour or so on the chimney pot he rarely appeared until it was time for his evening feed. However, almost from the moment the colonel and Dorothy appeared on the croft I became aware of his hovering presence.

'Hello, Gulliver!' I greeted him, and automatically hunched my shoulders ready for his landing, but to my consternation instead of coming to me he chose to land on the colonel's completely bald head. There was an enraged shout from the colonel and an equally enraged squawk from Gulliver as he was thrust roughly away. With screaming protestations he flew some distance away, only to return instantly to fly round and round as if preparing to repeat the manoeuvre.

'I'm so sorry,' I faltered apologetically. 'It's my pet gull. I should have warned you but I didn't think he would take any notice of you.' I tried hard to keep my countenance and my voice suitably serious, but the sight of the colonel, both hands clamped firmly over his bald head, dodging and feinting so as to be out of range of further assault, was too much for me. My voice broke into a choke of laughter which could not be disguised even by an assumed attack of coughing. I caught Dorothy's eye and the next moment we were both convulsed with a mirth that not even the truculent glare of her husband could wither.

'Infernal gull!' he muttered testily, though I thought I perceived a slight softening of his expression.

'I call him Gulliver,' I said.

'Infernal Gulliver!' responded the colonel heatedly.

There was a definite feel of autumn in the air the following day and, after a 'pride of the morning' mist had lifted, it revealed a serenely blue sky chalked with wispy clouds under which the land lay clean and polished while the sea gurgled as it lapped up the sunshine. Not surprisingly, the colonel professed himself enthralled by the scene and after breakfast announced his intention of sitting outside to smoke a cigar and contemplate his surroundings.

'Watch out for Gulliver, dear,' cautioned Dorothy. Her husband replied with a grim smile as he pulled a sturdy deerstalker hat firmly over his bald head. Dorothy and I washed up the dishes while we exchanged the sort of cosy news which people who have not met since childhood enjoy sharing. We saw the colonel carry a deck-chair over to a sequestered spot where he sat relaxing for a few minutes before taking out a cigar. There was, it seemed, an eddy of breeze outside which hampered the lighting of the cigar and he used several matches without apparent success. It then appeared that having exhausted his supply of matches he was rooting in his pocket for a second box, and while he was thus occupied Gulliver came into sight, flying investigatively over his chair. I can only surmise that the cigar in the colonel's mouth appeared to Gulliver like a stick or a clothes peg, for the next moment he touched down briefly on the deerstalker, swiftly plucked at the cigar and with a triumphant squawk flew away with it towards the far end of the croft. We saw the colonel shake his fist as he lunged after the gull. We saw Gulliver drop the cigar, but long before his pursuer could reach him he had retrieved it and flown with it out over the sea. In the kitchen we tried to stifle our laughter sufficiently to commiserate with the colonel when he came storming back to the cottage.

'That infernal gull of yours!' he charged me. 'He's stolen one of my best cigars. Just whipped it out of my mouth while I was sitting there, would you believe it?'

We assured him that we did believe it, having just witnessed the incident.

'But, darling,' soothed his wife, though her voice was taut with laughter, 'just think what a tale you'll have to tell at the club when you get back home. An encounter with a cigar-smoking seagull. You'll be able to dine on it for months.'

The colonel huffed a few acrid-sounding comments, but his glare was not half so irate as his voice and I got the distinct impression he was secretly amused by the incident. Sensing our inward laughter he soon retreated upstairs where, so Dorothy reported, he enjoyed a cigar in the safety of his bedroom.

During the next few days we came to suspect that Gulliver had either selected the colonel as a likely playmate or, for some obscure reason, had determined on a campaign of harassment, for whenever he ventured outdoors during daylight Gulliver would soon be hovering around, calling attention to his presence by picking up twigs and pebbles and dropping them recklessly close to wherever the colonel might be. If he was sitting in a deck-chair Gulliver would alight somewhere near by, make a rapid but stealthy approach, and begin an investigative pecking at his feet – a disagreeable experience for someone wearing no socks and flimsy sandals. So with many acerbic observations about women who treated birds as if they were brethren, the colonel, who normally liked to bare his head in the sunshine, took to wearing his deerstalker as a safety helmet to protect his head from Gulliver's several forms of bombardment; smoked his cigars indoors and when he ventured to take his siesta outdoors substituted more robust footwear for sandals. But Gulliver was not to be thwarted completely. Observing the colonel resting in his chair, he would take up his favourite perch on the chimney pot from whence he would indulge in a monotony of thin reedy shrieks which, according to the colonel, were as conducive to repose as would be the insistent ringing of a telephone bell.

There was no doubt that initially Gulliver's attentions affected the colonel's enjoyment of his holiday but as time went on he seemed to find them less of an annoyance, confiding to Dorothy that he found the gull's behaviour intriguing. Even when after much complicated negotiation he had managed to procure a current newspaper from the mainland, only to have Gulliver snatch it from his lap still unfolded and unread and scatter the pages over the croft, he had been more astounded than aggravated by the gull's behaviour.

But Gulliver's most inglorious misdemeanour was perpetrated towards the end of my friend's stay. It was a still day when the mushroomy smell of autumn lingered over the sun tinted moors; robins chirruped their territorial claims; spring-hatched cockerels practised their crowing and drifts of foraging starlings sped like dark shadows over the short grass of the hay-cleaned crofts. The weather being so mild, we were to lunch outdoors in the 'garden', which was the courtesy title for the small enclosure of land adjoining the cottage which I tried to protect from violation by my own and other people's cows and hens, and where I tried annually to grow the vegetables and flowers I missed so much, only, it seemed, then to have to sacrifice them just as regularly to the voracious appetite of the storms which wrenched them out of the ground long before the plants reached anything like maturity. But it was enclosed land and therefore to me it was a garden. We each took our tray and on each tray was a plate of bacon and eggs – smoked bacon, which I could not buy on the island and which had been specially ordered from the mainland, because I knew it was one of the colonel's favourite dishes. There was a wooden bench outside the cottage with room for two people to sit comfortably so I put down my tray on the grass.

'Will you watch my tray while I go indoors to get a stool?' I asked Dorothy. 'Don't for goodness' sake take your eyes off it in case Gulliver should be about.'

Ever gallant, the colonel put down his tray. 'Let me get the stool,' he insisted, and turning to his wife requested that she should similarly watch his tray. The stool was upstairs and while he went to get it I went quickly to the kitchen meat safe and took out a whole raw mackerel with the idea that if Gulliver did come to pester us the fish was large enough to keep him occupied while we enjoyed our meal. The colonel, now carrying the stool, stood courteously aside as I emerged from the kitchen with the fish. He was behind me as we reached the open door. His gasp of horror coincided with my own as we stood shocked into speechlessness at the sight of Dorothy, both arms waving protectively over two of the trays – hers and my own – while she stared helplessly at Gulliver who was helping himself to the final slice of bacon from the colonel's plate.

'Gulliver!' I bawled when I could find my voice.

'I did shout at him,' Dorothy rushed to explain. 'And I flipped my napkin at him but he wouldn't go away. It was impossible to protect all three trays at the same time.'

At that moment Gulliver caught sight of the mackerel I was holding in my hand and even in the split second it took for the bird to register the fact and form his intention I seemed to hear Ian Beag's voice, 'Supposin' they're full of food an' there comes a chance of something they like better they'll bring up everythin' that's in their stomachs just to make room for it,' Gulliver proceeded to demonstrate most convincingly that he preferred fresh mackerel to smoked bacon. He made room for it!

'Oh God!' murmured the colonel's wife, turning away from the resultant mess that had now been so neatly disgorged on to her husband's tray.

'Oh, Gulliver!' I expostulated, as he hopped over and snatched the mackerel from my grasp.

'Oh Glory be!' exclaimed the colonel, and to his eternal credit he put down the stool, sat on it and surrendered himself to great guffaws of body-shaking laughter.

It was not long after the colonel and Dorothy had returned home that Gulliver also made his farewell. By this time he was finding all the food he needed and as a consequence was spending more and more time beyond the area of the croft, and though he still returned regularly to be fed and also maintained his habit of subsequently squatting on the chimney pot I had accepted that the day of his desertion was not far off. When it came it was a day of hazy sunshine attended by a reticent breeze, and his going was in the nature of a valediction.

Early in the morning while feeding the hens I noticed an unusually large flock of young gulls close-circling the croft. All the gulls were identical in colouring and therefore in age to Gulliver and as the morning progressed the gathering of gulls increased until the air was clamorous with their squeaked invitations. Gulliver, having swallowed his morning fish, had taken up his chimney-pot perch from where he observed the other gulls with almost a detached air; sometimes answering them, though for a while it seemed that he was not disposed to join them. But watching him I could detect his yearning to belong; his growing intent; the urge for flight throbbing so compulsively through his restless wings that he had constantly to fold and refold them to his body. Then suddenly as I watched it seemed as if he could resist no longer and with rapturous squeals he flew up to mingle with the gyrating throng of his companions. My eyes followed him without difficulty at first, for even among so great a number of gulls he was easily identifiable by his superior size, but then, as if the flock were exultant at having enlisted their last reluctant member, their flight mounted higher and higher until they became a confusion against the clouds and I could no longer be sure which was Gulliver. I felt strangely bereft. I had been expecting him to leave. Indeed I would not have wished it otherwise, yet now at the moment of departure a swift surge of sadness sent me running inside for another mackerel which I held aloft while I called his name repeatedly in the hope he would return. But no matter how much I called and coaxed no gull came near. No gull detached itself from the throng or even swooped low to investigate and I wondered if, in the moment of decision to join his kind, the memory of the human who had nurtured him had been erased from his brain. Tired at last of holding up the fish I let my arm droop to my side and stood disconsolately watching the haphazard crowd of gulls achieving a rough formation as they flew round and round the croft in a semblance of a game of 'follow my leader'. I wondered if the leader was Gulliver. Once, twice and then a third time they circled before heading in the direction of the hills. I continued to watch them until the whole flock were merely scattered flecks in the sky which soon merged and then vanished altogether in the misty clouds that shrouded the sun. It was Gulliver's final leave-taking and to my knowledge I never saw him again.

Erchy assured me that gulls do not journey more than a few miles from their birthplaces until they are fully mature and I was rather inclined to accept his assurance, since shortly after Gulliver's departure there came a report that late campers at a site only about four miles away were having trouble with a gull which haunted their camp and had not only stolen their breakfast bacon on more than one occasion but had tried to snatch a pipe out of a man's mouth.

'Indeed, I do believe it must be that gull you reared yourself, surely,' said Morag. 'The one that military man that was stayin' with you used to say was his inferno.'

7
Tinker Tales

'DIRECTLY the dew is off the grass I believe it will make a good day for the corn-gathering,' Morag announced. It was indeed a good day for almost any outside work, the scarves of morning mist having been dissipated by fine spun autumn sunlight tempered by a soft breeze which would, in Morag's words, 'Drink the sweat from us as we worked.' I wrapped a clean tea towel round a fruit cake which I had baked the previous day and handed it to Morag, assuring her that as soon as I returned from milking I would be ready to begin work.

In England one thinks of corn as being wheat or maize; the basic ingredients of our daily bread and, watching even a mechanized corn harvest and smelling the clean zesty smell of the golden grain, one's imagination is ready to leap forward, evoking the nutty aroma of fresh wholewheat flour as it pours from the mill; the warm hunger-making smell of good fresh bread. In Bruach where soil and climate made the growing of wheat and maize impractical the term 'corn' referred to the sturdier oats and since the ultimate fate of the sheaves of oats was to be beaten against or with a stone so as to dislodge the grain for feeding to the poultry, the rest, the empty ears and the straw, being fed to the cattle, the crop evoked no such satisfying images.

Of course this had not always been so. Many Bruachites remembered the days when the corn crop had been threshed and winnowed on the croft and Morag herself had more than once referred to the nightly ritual of toasting the fresh grain over the open fire before feeding it into the quernstones; turning the quernstones with a stick inserted into a socket in the upper stone and grinding the corn ready for the next morning's porridge. Some of the old women remembering only too well the labour involved spoke of those times with a tinge of bitterness, but Morag seemed only to reflect sadly that porridge neither smelled nor tasted like real porridge any more.

When I presented myself at Morag's croft Ruari and Erchy had already fitted the wire 'corn-gathers' to their scythes and had begun work. Following in their wake I joined Morag and Janet in gathering up the fallen scythe-sweeps of corn and separating them into slim sheaves which we then tied with a twist of oat stalks. I had but little experience of making sheaves and that experience had led me to regard it as one of the more exacting tasks of the croft, since not only had the sheaves to be more or less uniform in girth – Morag had me almost counting the stalks so constant were her injunctions against making the sheaves too fat or too thin – but properly, the confusion of stalks had to be bunched with the ears lying tidily together and the ends butting trimly. In my efforts to comply with my tutor's instructions I found myself cradling each sheaf on my left arm as I might cradle an infant while with the right hand and forearm I coaxed and pushed at the stalks until they were all lying tolerably level. Then I tied them and meekly submitted them for scrutiny. Deft sheaf-making needs much practice and despite the excellent counselling my sheaves lying among those made by Morag and Janet were too readily identifiable by their lack of symmetry. The two women generously cloaked their amused dismay with occasional commendation which, though spurious, was clearly intended as encouragement; the two men took far less trouble to disguise their ridicule and to my ears even the breeze itself as it whispered through the new-cut swathes sounded as if it was having difficulty in suppressing its chuckles.

We worked on steadily, almost soundlessly save for our own voices and the mutterings of a few monitoring gulls who hovered so close Morag declared that we could almost speak to them. Once we halted for a quick strupak which Behag brought out to us but then we were back at work, and just as the men kept up the rhythm of their scythe strokes so did our bodies continue to stoop and straighten, stoop and straighten as we gathered and tied the sheaves before upending them in threes so they would shed the rain. My back ached; my arms and neck and even my cheeks were rasped by the rough corn stalks and fretted by the wind and sun; fragments of chaff had worked their way into my eyes and my feet were lacerated by the spiky stubble thrusting through my flimsy sandals. But since there was a tacit determination that the corn harvest once begun must be finished by sunset – God and the weather permitting – we allowed ourselves no respite save perhaps briefly when Ruari and Erchy, pausing to sharpen a scythe, made some comment which seemed to justify a moment's consideration before a reply was given. Then we took the opportunity to relax for a fleeting moment or two, throwing back our heads to let the breeze cool our necks and pressing the palms of our hands hard against our backs in an effort to push the aches from our bones. However, if we prolonged the pause the men quickly began to taunt us on our idleness or to chide us mockingly for shirking to which Janet and Morag retorted with equal derision that their inexpert scything was making our task more difficult. Indignation on both sides soon gave way to banter and banter to laughter which temporarily shook the tiredness from our bodies and stimulated us to further effort.

At last the scythe strokes ceased almost with the suddenness of a clock stopping and straightening up we saw there was no corn left standing. There was a moment of silence as we stood surveying the stubble and on the flushed, moist faces of my companions there was an expression of contentment that the mellowing sunlight lit almost to ecstasy. Ruari took out his pipe and Erchy lit a cigarette and while Morag and Janet and I finished tying the remaining sheaves the two men murmured together assessing the yield of corn.

'You have plenty corn, I'm thinkin',' Ruari called to Morag.

'Aye,' admitted Morag cautiously. 'I believe I have so supposin' the rain will keep away until I have it stacked just.'

Ruari treated her to a disparaging glance. In Bruach there was a precept that corn must be left standing for three Sundays in the field before it could be considered dry enough to be built into a winter stack and the possibility that Bruach could be without rain for close on three weeks he considered too remote for spoken contempt.

The men picked up their scythes and resting them over their shoulders returned with Morag to the cottage for their well-earned strupak. Janet and I stayed to up-end the remaining sheaves.

'Well that's finished for a whiley,' Janet said when the last sheaf had been set up. She flexed her shoulders, 'And the Dear knows I'm that tired, I feel as if I'm not worth a docken at the end of it,' she added, and ended with a chuckle in case her remark should be construed as the beginning of a grumble. Taking off her work apron, she bundled it under her arm and moved off in the direction of the cottage.

There was by now a gentle coolness in the breeze which was doing much to anaesthetize the smarting of my skin and despite my own desire for a strupak so satisfying was the contemplation of the day's task completed that I wanted to linger and enjoy the sense of repose which seemed to be settling over the cornfield much as if the land having yielded its bounty was, like the reapers, preparing to relax. On the pretext of emptying my sandals of grain and chaff, I lagged behind and for a few snatched moments stood enjoying the slow throb of happiness that comes when a tedious job is finally disposed of; remembering the growing corn combed by the breeze into green strands across the plot; savouring the fresh straw-scented air; the sight of new corn stubble polished to brilliance by the tawny sunlight; the stooked corn sheaves which with their shaggy heads leaning together and skirts spread to catch the breeze reminded me of trios of little girls sharing some whispered secret.

'Indeed have you no' seen enough of the corn for the day or are you wantin' to take it to bed with you?' Janet's voice interrupted my thoughts and I hurried to join her.

The men's scythes were hooked over the limb of a dead tree near Morag's cottage proclaiming their owners' presence in the kitchen where we found them drinking tea and eating wedges of the cake I had given to Morag that morning.

'Are you no goin' to sit down yourself an' take a strupak?' protested Morag when I made no attempt to join them.

'Just a cup in my hand,' I said using the Bruach idiom. 'Then I must be away.' There was already a faint edge of twilight creeping above the mainland hills and with the hens to be fed and Bonny to be milked I was loth to sit down for fear of being unable to coax my weary limbs into functioning again.

'Then you'll take a piece of your own cake, surely?' Morag pressed. I shook my head. There were fresh mackerel fillets waiting to be cooked for my supper and I wanted no cake to take the edge off my appetite.

'It's good this,' said Erchy reaching for the last slice.

'Of course it is,' I replied archly.

'An' tell me now, did you bake this cake in the tin the old tinker made for you?' asked Morag.

'I did,' I acknowledged, 'but if I'd known yesterday that you were planning to gather in your corn today I would have baked a bigger one for you. Erchy himself could easily eat the whole of that.'

'I would so if I got the chance,' agreed Erchy.

'Whist!' Morag admonished. 'Indeed but I'm well pleased with what you gave me,' she said, 'but what I'm sayin' now is that it's as well you got the old tinker to make the tin for you when you did for he'll make no more.'

'Why not?' I demanded.

'Mo ghaoil,' she responded, 'did you no hear he's passed on this three weeks back?'

'He's dead?' The old tinker was by way of being a friend of mine and I felt slightly indignant that no one had spoken to me of his death until now.

'He is so,' she confirmed.

'Accident or old age?' I probed.

'No accident nor age but a tumulus on the brain,' Morag explained. 'They took him away to hostapol on the mainland but he didn't wait long there before he was gone.'

'I don't believe he thought much of hospitals anyway, no nor doctors either,' Erchy observed. 'Tinkers don't as a rule.'

'No, I believe you're right about that,' I agreed, and suppressed a reminiscent grin.

The old tinker used to visit Bruach periodically, selling his water dippers and milk pails, and he was usually accompanied by a tiny woman whom he referred to as his 'small wee body' or sometimes less dotingly as 'the body' and who I surmised was his wife. They were a curious pair; he with a face tanned to the colour of liver sausage, roguishly glinting eyes and thick lips that only loosely enclosed a tongue that I knew well could spill out piety and profanity, flattery and execration with a similar degree of neutrality and expertise. The 'small wee body', on the other hand, was pale and timid-looking, her thin mouth constantly sucked into a virtuous pucker that was puzzlingly belied at times by a merry glint in her eyes. The old man, according to Morag, was one of the few genuine tinkers still roaming the island, though many Bruachites disputed her assertion, arguing that only the 'small wee body' was genuinely Highland the old man being 'more than a leg an' a half Irish'. Moreover, they claimed that his pails and dippers were not his own work but were purchased from ironmongers on the mainland, the tinker supplying only his trademark of a 'strengthening' dribble of solder around the base so as to fool people into thinking they were buying genuine 'tinker-made'. But whether they were genuinely 'tinkered' or not, the Bruachites still bought his pails and dippers and apparently found no cause for dissatisfaction. I too had used his pails and dippers and also on one occasion I had at Morag's suggestion asked the old man to fashion for me a cake tin of a size which I had found it impossible to buy in any of the mainland shops or from any mail order catalogue. The reason I required such a 'bespoke' tin was for making Victoria sandwich cakes of which I am extremely fond, and the best sandwich cake I happen to believe is one that has been baked in a single tin deep enough to allow for a cake to be cut through the middle before being sandwiched together with filling. Sandwich cakes baked in the recommended two shallow tins never in my opinion turn out to have quite the delectable moistness of texture which I always find so irresistible. At the time I possessed only one tin which was of suitable depth but unfortunately it was too large in diameter and as a consequence unless there were sufficient 'droppers-in' for strupaks the cake would grow stale before I could consume the half of it. Resolving therefore to put the old tinker to the test, I told him of my problem, gave him the approximate measurements of the tin I wanted him to make for me, and waited to see what would happen.

I was in the middle of baking when next he called and wiping the dough from my hands I went to answer his summons of, 'Are ye within there, mam?' shouted through the open door. Lifting an arm with its shining cluster of milk pails in salute, he acknowledged my appearance with easy confidence. Beside him stood the 'small wee body', who was diffidently offering for my inspection a shiny round tin which at first glance appeared to be exactly what I wanted.

'Oh, you've made it for me! How splendid!' I exclaimed delightedly, but as soon as I took the tin from her and examined it more closely my enthusiasm waned. Undoubtedly it was genuinely 'tinker-made'. Even without the well-known lion trademark which decorated the bottom the number of joins would have proclaimed the fact irrefutably. I wondered how many island scrap heaps had been raided to provide the raw materials for the tin. Pleasure gave way to dismay when closer scrutiny revealed that the base was made up of three separate pieces of tin joined by 'seams' which, when I turned the tin over, I saw were secured by what, even to my untrained eye, looked to be excessively shaky-handed dribbles of solder. I imagined that unless the tin was first lined with paper any cake baked in it would have to be scraped out rather than turned out.

'Will it stand heat?' I asked dubiously, turning the tin over and over.

'Indeed, mam, supposin' you was to put that tin

in a fire oven and bake it, it would come out as good as new,' he assured me with nimble complacency.

'Well, that is the idea,' I reminded him. 'I want it for baking cakes, not feeding the hens.'

If there was a flicker of consternation in his eyes it was succeeded within the space of a blink by a look of utter guilelessness. 'God's truth, mam!' he ejaculated, ''tis the lazy tongue of me that's given you the wrong word for it. What I'm trying to say is, mam, that that tin wouldn't crack at the sight of a furnace.' He turned to his companion. '"The body" here will tell you that now.'

'The body's' attention had been momentarily diverted by a moo from Bonny who was tethered further down the croft and I had a fleeting though perhaps false impression that his foot had moved furtively in her direction, startling her into response. 'Oh, indeed, mam, a furnace,' she corroborated instantly in a voice that was barely more audible than the sound of a brush sweeping over a polished floor and, still not satisfied with my reaction, she emphasized, 'A hot furnace, mam. Sure the hotter the better for that one.' She was looking at the old man as she spoke and it crossed my mind that perhaps he would indeed stand more heat than the tin he had made for me. In any case since 'small wee body' reputedly had never lived in anything more substantial than a sod and tarpaulin hut with an open fire and a hole in the roof through which the smoke escaped, her experience of cake-baking was likely to have been severely limited and her assurances therefore could carry little conviction. However, since I had asked the tinker to make the tin especially for me I felt I had no alternative but to purchase it from him. At least, I told myself, I had a genuine 'tinker-made' tin and even if, as seemed likely, it was unsuitable for cake-baking at least it would be a source of interest and curiosity to my friends.

Fearing I might have hurt the old man's feelings by showing my misgivings about his handiwork, I tried to atone by quite unnecessarily buying myself one of his dippers.

'There's no doubt your dippers are good and strong,' I complimented him as I handed over the money for the dipper and the baking tin.

'Indeed everything I'm after makin' is good an' strong, just as you say, mam,' he acknowledged complacently. 'I have two sons that's the same way; captains in the army both of them an' where else would they be gettin' their strength now if it wasn't from me?' He inclined a deprecatory nod towards 'the body', who undid her mouth and tried a tentative smile. 'No, mam,' he went on, 'I need to give my work strength or folks would be after complainin' an' I would be for loosin' my livin', would I not?' He lifted the lid off one of the milk pails and producing a filthy rag wrapped the money in it before replacing it in the pail and pressing the lid back firmly. 'No indeed, mam,' he reiterated. 'It wouldn't pay me not to take care when I'm doin' my job. A tinker's not like a doctor that can just bury his mistakes.'

As he and 'the body' turned to go there came another 'moo' from Bonny.

'Is your beast near calvin' then?' he asked.

Though all Bruach cattle were out on the moors

at this time of year a cow approaching calving would normally be brought in and tethered on the croft thus enabling her to have a bite of good grass and also enabling the owner to keep a better eye on her in case of difficulty, hence the old man's question.

'No,' I told him. 'I brought her in because she has something the matter with her eye and as the vet is supposed to be visiting the village today I want her close at hand so I can ask him to have a look at her.'

'Bloody hell, mam!' he exclaimed genially. 'You'll be excusin' me surely but why would you be needin' a vet now for to cure a sore eye in a cow? Sure I can cure her myself in no time at all.' He darted an enquiring glance at me. 'Will I get to try?' he asked.

'You will,' I told him. I was happy enough to let the old man try his skill since it was by no means certain the vet would be able to reach Bruach that day and tinkers are regarded as being good folk doctors. Many were the stories told in Bruach of a tinker effecting a cure in an animal or even a human when the vet or the doctor were alleged to have been nonplussed. The old people of Bruach also had a good knowledge of folk medicine when they could be induced to confide it but on the whole they were reticent about offering their knowledge except in general discussion at the ceilidhs by which time the symptoms had usually disappeared or the patient was dead. At first I had put their tight-lipped attitude down to their fear of being derided by the younger folk, many of whom had by now come to share the professional ridicule of homely remedies.

But of course I may have been wrong; it may have been only their conception of clan loyalty that kept their lips sealed for everyone has to earn a living and after all many of the clan were qualified vets or doctors; some were even undertakers!

I led the old man towards Bonny and she, catching sight of us, lifted up her head from grazing the good grass of the croft and watched us expectantly. She looked pathetic with her one eye half-closed and dribbling pus but she herself seemed to be suffering no discomfort.

'I believe 'tis no more than a sharp bit of heather stem that has got itself under the eyelid,' said the tinker as he approached. Bonny shook her horns at him threateningly but his response was to grip one of her horns firmly the better to examine her eye.

'It's all right, Bonny,' I assured her, and because he was in my company she made no more gestures of protest.

'Will she take a wee potach?' asked the tinker.

'She'll take as many as I want to give her,' I assured him.

'Aye, well see an' bring a wee potach for her,' he instructed.

I left him and 'the body' still discussing Bonny and going over to the cottage made up a potach. When I returned the old tinker was chewing vigorously at what I thought at first was a quid of tobacco but as he opened his mouth to speak to me I saw that whatever he was chewing was leaking green juice which ran down his chin as he spoke.

'Did you get the potach?' he asked.

I took it from my pocket and seeing it Bonny moved

forward. 'Now don't give it to her yet just,' the tinker ordered as he moved up to within a foot of Bonny's head and bent down. Resting his hand on her neck and staring straight into her eye he said quietly, 'Offer her the potach now but hold it just out of her reach so she cannot get it. Make her strain for it just.'

I did as I was bid and Bonny's eyes opened wide with impatient greed as she strained to reach the potach. At the precise moment when she was engrossed with reaching for it, the old tinker gathered all the spittle and juice in his mouth and spat expertly straight into Bonny's eye. I am not sure whether it was Bonny or myself who recoiled the more violently from the sudden expectoration but it was Bonny who recovered herself more quickly. She screwed up her sore eye and tossed her head, but she was not deterred from reaching for the potach and taking advantage of my momentary inaction she took it from my unyielding fingers.

'That's the way of it,' pronounced the tinker with great satisfaction. 'Likely she'll be the better of that.' He wiped his green-stained lips and chin on his sleeve. 'I'm thinkin' you'll no be needin' the vet to her now.'

'What was it you were chewing?' I asked.

He nodded at 'the body' who unclenched her hand to show me a few sprigs of ground ivy which she still held.

'And you reckon that will cure her?'

'I do so, mam. You will see her eye as good as new in a day or so,' he assured me.

There was the sound of a car engine and a few

minutes later the vet came striding towards us. He summed up the situation at once. 'You've been having a go at faith-healing, have you?' he said, dismissing my embarrassment with a lenient smile. 'What have you been up to, then?'

Readily the old tinker explained the treatment. The vet listened attentively. 'Aye, well,' he said when the old man had finished. 'Let's leave it at that and see what happens. I have to come out again tomorrow to see Johnny Tom's cow so if your cure doesn't show signs of working we can try mine.'

'I've never seen it fail yet,' said the tinker. 'Not on man nor beast.' He turned towards 'the body'. 'Look now but didn't I do the same thing for herself a while back an' not a sign of trouble since.' 'The body' released a sad smile. 'But you must make sure it comes as a shock to them,' the tinker went on. 'What you must do first is tell some tale they're goin' to find it hard to believe an' when they're starin' at you with their eyes so wide they can't open any wider then that's the moment you spit.'

The vet slanted a look of stealthy amusement at me. 'What tale did you tell your wife to get her to open her eyes wide enough?' he asked the old man.

'Ach, I told her I was swearin' off the whisky for a week,' came the reply, followed by a guffaw of laughter.

When the tinker and the 'small wee body' had gone the vet turned his attention to Bonny. 'Seriously, what do you want to do about her?' he asked. 'Myself, I don't mind telling you I'd like to see how the spit cure works.'

'To be honest I'd like to see that too,' I admitted.

'But I don't want to risk the eye perhaps getting worse.'

'Oh, I don't think there's much fear of that,' he comforted. 'Anyway I'll look in next time I'm down just to make sure.' Back at the car he said, 'I can't help being amused by this because my wife has had a sore eye for two or three days now. She got some drops from the doctor but they don't seem to be doing much good. It came into my mind when the tinker was telling us about curing his wife.'

'You're going to try the same cure on your wife?'

'I'll have to think of a good tale to tell her first,' he said with a secret smile.

'Why not?' I asked, joining in his laughter.

'The trouble is I'd never know whether or not it worked.'

'Why not?' I repeated fatuously.

'Why not? Because if I tried that treatment on my wife I wouldn't have a wife any more. She'd be up and away on the first boat,' he told me. 'And who'd blame her?'

The following morning Bonny's eye was so much improved that when the vet called later in the afternoon he professed himself perfectly satisfied with her progress. 'In fact,' he said seriously, 'I cannot do better than recommend you to continue the treatment.'

I burst out laughing. 'No damty fear!' I said, but my amusement began to border on agitation as I realized there was no reciprocal laughter from the vet. 'You're joking!' I accused him, studying his face while waiting for the hint of a smile to betray itself. 'You are, aren't you,' I faltered.

The vet returned my stare steadily. 'No, I'm not,' he replied, and though his mouth relaxed into a smile his voice was firm.

'Look!' I laughed protestingly, 'I can't go chewing weeds and spitting them into cows' eyes.'

'Why not?' he retorted. 'If a simple remedy like that will do the trick why bother with anything more complicated?'

I looked from him to Bonny. 'But surely she's so much better it's very likely the one treatment will suffice,' I prevaricated, still half convinced he was teasing.

'That could be,' he admitted. 'But supposing it doesn't then you'll be wanting something from me to clear it up and neither of us will ever know whether or not the tinker's cure was truly effective.'

Bewilderedly I accepted his reasoning.

'Cheer up!' he bade me in parting. 'It's good to live and learn.'

'You're a sadist,' I told him, and was sure I detected a gleam of pure devilment in his eyes as he drove away.

The following morning I dutifully gathered a bunch of ground ivy and chewed with steadily increasing distaste until my mouth was full of green pap which was about as palatable as a mixture of soap and mustard. Then with purpose in mind and a potach in my hand I approached the tethered Bonny. As before she espied the potach; as before her eyes widened with greedy anticipation as she reached for it. It was going to be easy, I told myself, and mustering the contents of my mouth I prepared to spit. But at the crucial moment a horse-fly must have bitten Bonny's side and as she swung her head round to attack it she caught me with the tip of a horn, knocking me off balance, and making me stumble. When I picked myself up I stood gaping and panic-stricken at the dawning realization that the mouthful of green pap was no longer in my mouth; neither was it in Bonny's eye. At the moment of stumbling I had swallowed the whole wretched mess! I clutched at my throat. Having no idea what effect ground ivy might have on the digestion of a human, it seemed there was only one thing to do. I put my finger down my throat and retched.

According to Culpepper, ground ivy 'easeth all griping pains, windy and choleric humours in the stomach, spleen or belly, helps the yellow jaundice by opening the stoppings of the gall and liver, and melancholy by opening the stoppings of the spleen; expelleth venom or poison and also the plague; it provokes urine and women's courses'.

The old tinker's remedy certainly cured Bonny's eye and I reckoned I too should be healthy enough for a time. The cake tin he had made for me was also an enormous success, the cakes cooking to perfection and sliding out effortlessly when done. It proved so useful, in fact, that I resolved to ask him to make me another one. Now it seemed I was too late. I wondered what had become of the 'small wee body'.

'Ach, didn't she go away to the hostapol with him an' now folks say she's after makin' her home with her son on the mainland.'

'Her son – and the old man's?' I queried.

'Aye, I believe he's one of them scrap tinks.'

I smiled. 'The old man told me he had two sons and they were "captains in the army both".'

Ruari let out a scornful grunt of laughter. 'I wonder which army that would be?'

'Not the Salvation Army anyway,' said Erchy. 'I'm damty sure none of his sons would ever be sober enough to join that.'

'The flea army, maybe,' murmured Janet.

'Indeed if I'd told as many lies as that man I couldn't face myself,' Ruari declared with a shake of his head.

'Lies or no, where will we be after gettin' as good dippers an' pails now he's gone?' asked Morag, who frequently betrayed a soft spot for the island tinkers. Tinkers on the mainland she was willing to concede might 'steal the eyes out of your head an' come back for the sockets' but not island tinkers: their behaviour was gentlemanly in comparison.

'Right enough we'll miss the old man's pails and dippers,' said Janet.

'And his "small wee body",' I said. 'We'll miss her too.'

'Not so much as the barman at the bar will miss her, I'm thinkin',' said Ruari.

'He'll miss the pair of them,' said Erchy.

'Did she drink too?' I asked innocently. It was accepted in Bruach that tinkers got roaring drunk but I found it hard to associate drunkenness with the meek little 'body'.

'Drink?' echoed Erchy. 'Too damty true she drank. I've seen her myself take six good drams one after the other an' still by the look of her you'd swear she'd never touched a drop.'

'The woman!' ejaculated Janet disapprovingly.

'Aye, it's true right enough,' Ruari confirmed. 'But when she'd be takin' another three or four on top of the six then the barman would have to watch out for fear she would be fightin' her way in.'

'In where?' I asked.

'Into the bar,' explained Erchy. 'See, the old tinker wouldn't allow her in with him so he'd take whisky out to her. He thought by doin' this he'd stop her havin' too much. But ach, he used to get so drunk himself he couldn't remember how many she would be havin'. So long as there was money to pay for it he'd buy it. By God! she used to get real savage with him at times wantin' to get inside.'

I felt slightly dazed. The frail little 'small wee body' turning out to be a drunken virago? 'I'd have expected nine whiskies to have put her flat on her back for a week,' I said.

Ruari chortled. 'How many drams it needed to do that to her I wouldn't be knowin',' he admitted. 'But I doubt when she'd taken them the old tinker would be best pleased there wasn't much of a size to her seein' it was himself would have to carry her back to their place.'

'Oh, the Dear!' observed Janet, utterly failing to conceal her amusement.

'Carry her? Did she truly become as incapable as that?' I wanted to know.

'Sure enough,' Erchy asserted. 'Limp as an old coat she'd be an' many's the time I've seen him sling her over his shoulder an' go off with her after the bar was closed for the night.'

'Aye, an' himself that drunk he would be weavin'

about like tangle in the tide,' agreed Ruari. 'Mind you, he must have been good to her or he would have just left her there.'

'It's a terrible long way back from the bar to their hut,' Morag pointed out.

'Ach, I don't suppose he'd carry her that far,' said Erchy. 'Just far enough for the sake of appearances I reckon an' then he'd throw her at the side of the road. She'd keep there well enough till she would be makin' her own way.'

I looked at him with raised eyebrows. 'It's as true as I'm here,' he assured me. 'Tinks don't care, just.'

8

Rowan

'AYE, she's a fine lassie right enough,' said Tearlaich, his shrewd glance flicking over the sturdy, full-bosomed young tourist as if he was assessing her for carcass weight rather than charm or beauty.

Tearlaich and I had met outside the Post Office where I, having finished my business, was waiting while Morag got her paraffin can filled when we could walk home together.

'An' who would it be you are after sayin' is a fine lassie?' asked Morag, joining us at that moment.

Tearlaich nodded towards the receding figure of the young woman. 'That one from Glasgow that Lachy's so mad keen about,' he told her.

Morag put down her heavy can the better to study the tourist. 'Lachy's a rascal,' she pronounced.

I shot her an amused glance. While her own nephew Hector's philanderings with women might have been described as rascally by those who did not understand his benevolent attentions to women, I hardly thought the normally reticent Lachy deserved the epithet.

'I strikes me he's head over heels in love with the girl,' I said.

'An' so he is,' agreed Morag. 'See, she's kind of different from the lassies hereabouts, so it makes a nice change for him.' She smiled indulgently. 'Indeed he's fairly enjoyin' himself is Lachy.'

From my own observations I would have thought the love affair between Lachy and the tourist was more intense than Morag was prepared to admit. I said, 'I wonder if it will be just a holiday romance or if eventually they'll get married?'

Morag had bent to pick up her paraffin can but my question startled her into uprightness. 'Marrit?' she repeated, and she and Tearlaich exchanged swift glances of understanding. 'Lachy will no' be marryin' her at all, mo ghaoil,' she stated positively, and seeing my expression shook her head and added more emphatically. 'Never while the Lord spares him.'

'He'll find it hard enough to marry her if the Lord doesn't spare him,' said Tearlaich.

'Why won't he marry her?' I asked.

'What use would be a lassie like that to Lachy?' demanded Morag in reply.

I smiled uncertainly. 'But surely when young people are in love they're not going to assess what use one is going to be to the other. They're in love and that's all they care about.'

'Love,' mocked Morag. In the Gaelic language there are many words which express affection of the deepest kind and I could never understand why, when I used the English word 'love', the Bruachites appeared to be stricken with an embarrassment which they attempted to conceal with ridicule. 'Love doesn't milk the cattle an' rear the calves an' work the peats an' cook the potatoes,' Morag went on to explain. 'In this place a man wants a woman to work beside him.'

From my experience the men of Bruach wanted their women not just to work beside them but to work instead of them if it could be managed but I forbore from saying so.

'She could learn all these things,' I argued, though I did not remind her of my own apprenticeship.

'Not someone from Glasgow,' refuted Morag, 'not unless she had the Highlands in her blood.'

'But,' I pointed out, 'look at that man in Keppoch who brought home a bride from Glasgow . . .'

'Her that wouldn't learn to milk a cow nor cut a peat in all the time she was marrit to him?' interrupted Morag scathingly.

'They were a happy family,' I insisted.

'They were so, till he died,' she admitted. 'An' didn't he die long before he needed to through workin' so hard doin' her share as well as his own?' She turned to Tearlaich. 'Was that not the way of it, Tearlaich?'

'That was the way of it,' supported Tearlaich absentmindedly. He was still looking towards the distant figure of the young tourist. 'I'm thinkin' if Lachy plans to marry that one she'll not be wantin' to keep the feast till the weddin' night,' and added after a slight pause: 'All the same, if he's not careful he might land himself with a Miss Wade the same as Hamish.'

In the days of her comparative youth Miss Wade had made her first visit to Bruach and had fallen in love with the then-handsome Hamish and for thirty-five years now, so the Bruachites claimed, she had been returning every year to Bruach for her holidays with the hope that some day Hamish would ask her to marry him.

'Oh, right enough Hamish made a great fuss of her like the men does over any lassie that comes from the town,' Morag had said when she told me the story. 'But then Hamish was certain she would be goin' back to her own home an' her own kind an' he wasn't likely to see her again. But ach, though he was surprised when she came back the next year he didn't think much of it so the two of them passed the time together. He got a bit of a shock when she came back the next year an' the next an' when folks started teasin' him as to what Miss Wade had in mind he took the fright of his life at the woman an' he's been tryin' to keep out of her way since.

'She still comes, though,' I had pointed out, 'and Hamish is still a bachelor. Maybe they will make a match of it some day.'

'Never till two Sabbaths meets,' Morag had reiterated. 'At the age she is now a man wouldn't be wantin' her for warmin' his bed, let alone tryin' to teach her the ways of the croft.'

To be fair I believe Miss Wade had tried her hand at milking cows and cutting peats and working in the hay. Whether her efforts had shown too little promise or whether she herself had found the tasks too distasteful was a matter for surmise, but certainly I had never seen her within shouting distance of a cow byre or a peat hag or even on the croft when there was work to be done. According to the crofter widow with whom she regularly stayed, after thirty-five holidays in Bruach Miss Wade had still not mastered the lighting of an oil lamp.

'Lachy's gey young to be thinkin' of marryin',' said Tearlaich, who at fifty plus was still only thinking about it.

I could not remember how old Lachy was but I did recall he had been old enough to vote at the last election three years previously, but of course in Bruach the age of thirty-five was regarded as being the ideal for marriage for both men and women, the reason being that their children would then be there to look after them in their old age.

'It doesn't take much thinkin' about to choose a Member of Parliament,' said Tearlaich, 'but a wife, now, that's different. . . .' He would no doubt have continued discoursing on the necessary attributes needed for a crofter's wife but our chat was interrupted by the noise of an engine and turning to look up the brae we saw the carrier's lorry breasting the hill.

'I wonder will he have my tar?' said Tearlaich, as with unexpected gallantry he picked up Morag's can. 'I'll take this as far as the lorry,' he offered. 'We'll likely get a lift down the brae with him.'

'I hope he's bringing something for me,' I said, and could not have known how prophetic were my words.

'That would be your mirror, likely?' asked Morag.

I nodded. Hoping to improve the appearance of my small kitchen and give the effect of more light I had some weeks earlier ordered a fairly large wall mirror from a store on the mainland. Two weeks previously I had received notification from the railway company that a package awaited me at the station. Now I was fairly confident that the mirror would be on the carrier's lorry.

The carrier's first words confirmed my hopes. 'I have a "glass with care" for you, Miss Peckwitt,' he called as he stopped the lorry beside us.

'Oh, good! I do hope it's not broken,' I exclaimed.

The driver looked affronted. 'If she is she was broken before I put a hand on her,' he said.

It happened too often that breakable things were already broken by the time they reached Bruach and I had cogitated for some time before committing myself to ordering the mirror. It would have been much less risky if I could have gone to the mainland and brought the mirror back in my car, but the care of the animals tied me to the croft and I knew it might be a year or more before I could make the trip. Unlike the Hebrideans, who believed that 'hope deferred' was good practice because it ultimately quelled desire, my own temperament led me to endorse the old proverb that 'hope deferred maketh the heart sick'. Having set my heart on a mirror for the kitchen, I wanted it as speedily as possible, so, after balancing the risks of its journey by rail and carrier against the frustration of waiting, I ordered the mirror, stressing to the suppliers the innumerable hazards of the journey and appealing to them to pack it with extreme care. I knew, of course, the mirror would be insured against breakage *en route* but insurance is little recompense for the abyss of disappointment one feels when one unpacks a much-anticipated parcel only to find the contents shattered.

We climbed aboard the lorry, Morag and I in the cab beside the driver and Tearlaich perched on the load. At Tearlaich's cottage we dropped him, a large fifty-five-gallon drum of tar and a tin of paint; at other crofts along the way the driver unloaded more tar drums along with bags of meal; coils of rope and chains, and at Dugald's croft a small net-covered box containing a live puppy.

Dugald regarded the box with palpable annoyance. 'What's this?' he asked.

'What does it look like?' the carrier taxed him. 'You must have sent away for the dog, surely?'

'Indeed I did so a while back but I'm gettin' one now from Alistair Ruag over on Rhuna. I'm no wantin' to keep two dogs.' He began to turn away.

'You can take him an' send him back on the train tomorrow.'

'Hell, man!' protested the carrier, 'you'll have to take the beast now he's here.'

'Indeed I will not,' Dugald replied testily. 'Didn't I write to the man more than a week ago tellin' him not to send the dog seein' I got another?'

'You cannot have given him enough notice or surely he would not have taken the trouble to pay out good money to send it,' accused the carrier.

'That is a lie,' insisted Dugald, his testiness increasing. 'The man is wantin' to force me to take a beast he cannot get rid of any place else just.' Untying the net, he condescended to lift the small black and white bundle from the box by the scruff of the neck. The puppy stank of dung with which its hindquarters were caked and as Dugald surveyed it with dislike the puppy whimpered with terror. 'I reckon he'll no' be much good,' he said off-handedly as he replaced the puppy in the box. 'There's too much white on him for a start.'

Bruach sheepdogs were mostly black with perhaps a white throat and chest. A dog with too high a proportion of white in its colouring they believed was likely to have poor eyesight or to develop poor eyesight prematurely and be of little use for working hill sheep where it needed to see long distances.

The puppy did not whimper as I bent forward and lifted it gently on to my lap. 'I'll keep him,' I said.

Dugald's mouth fell open. 'Indeed you will no,' he said when he had recovered himself. 'Why would you be keepin' a sheep dog when you have no sheep?'

He made a derogatory sound in the back of his throat as he looked down and saw my hand resting protectively on the puppy. 'You'll be after makin' a pet of him just an' likely he'll get away from you an' be chasin' other folk's sheep.'

As in all sheep country Bruach had its problems with sheep-worrying dogs and I could well understand Dugald's fears but at that moment I was in no mood to allay them. Instead I smiled at him with a set, determined smile which I hope masked at least some of my real feelings. 'I'll keep him, Dugald,' I repeated. 'Just tell me how much they're asking for him and I'll either give Johnny, the bus driver, the money in the morning and then he can give it to you, or if you like you can tell me the address of the owner and I'll write to him direct.' I knew I was being high-handed but it was necessary that I should be so.

Dugald glared at me while the puppy, oblivious of the combat, bestowed a series of tiny-tongued caresses on my hand before turning himself round to nestle more deeply and trustingly in my lap. 'There's no need for either of us to argue any more,' I told Dugald.

'Indeed there is so!' he opposed authoritatively. 'It is myself the dog was sent to an' it is myself will be tellin' the carrier to take him back where he came from. It is best that the man who sent him should learn his lesson for fear he would be tryin' the same trick over again.'

I think I managed to continue smiling, though I suspect without a trace of affability. Dugald met my smile with a glowering silence. The seconds went by.

The carrier said, 'Will you be wantin' to keep the box or will I put it back on the lorry an' send it off to the mannie in the mornin'?'

'I shan't want it,' I told him. The puppy was not going to spend one more minute of his life in that nasty little box.

'The label says he answers to the name of Glen,' the carrier added as he threw the empty box on to the lorry and climbed into his seat.

Dugald was still regarding me from under his eyebrows. I suspected he was by no means averse to my keeping the puppy if only for the reason that to return him would mean Dugald having to pay the carrier for his trouble but to be openly defied by a woman was for him too much of an affront to be tolerated without resistance. He shuffled his feet and then spoke. 'The mannie is wantin' three pounds for him,' he yielded at last. 'Now you will see and be sure to give Johnny the money in the morning,' he stipulated, saving his face by pretending that the reason for his attitude was that he doubted my intention to pay for the puppy.

'Miss Peckwitt will do that right enough,' Morag was quick to assure him. There was a glint of triumph in her eyes and more than a trace of disapproval in her voice.

There followed an exchange in Gaelic between the carrier and Dugald; negotiations, exhortations and instructions about many things which could be so much better expressed in their own language and which in any case were no concern of mine. I let the conversation pass over my head and the puppy slept fitfully in my lap. At length the lorry driver let in the clutch and as the lorry started to move away instead of the scowling farewell I expected from Dugald I was offered a most cordial handshake. I got the impression he was mightily pleased with the result of at least one of his negotiations that day.

My decision to take the puppy, prompted as it had been by the plight of the poor little thing, was not so impulsive as it appears. As I wandered alone on the Bruach moors I often thought how rewarding the companionship of a faithful dog could be. I went alone not because I did not enjoy human company but because except when there was work to do the Bruachites themselves liked solitude for their moorland rambling and much as I looked forward to the visits of my town friends I confess that, except for a stroll on a fine evening, I was reluctant to invite them to share my 'wild wanders'. They were too insensitive, as undoubtedly I had been when I first came to Bruach, to have an eye for more than scenery; too lacking in comprehension of the ways of wild creatures. With me it had now become instinct to freeze the instant a flicker of unusual movement caught my eye but when I hissed at my town friends to keep completely still they invariably questioned why and twisted and turned their bodies in an effort to catch a glimpse of whatever I was seeing. 'Keep still!' I would command tersely. 'Move only your eyes and try to look where I am looking.' But more often than not, no matter how co-operative they intended to be, they would edge clumsily nearer and drive away anything that might have been of interest.

But a dog, trained to obey a command, would be different, I thought, though I had baulked at coming to a decision. I had once owned a wonderful dog; a devoted companion who seemed to sense and adapt himself to my every mood and the hurt when he died was so intense I resolved that never again would I 'give my heart to a dog to tear'. But today the decision seemed to have been thrust upon me and I recalled with a sense of satisfaction how the previous evening when I had been walking home from milking Bonny there had been a new moon, thin as a nail paring hanging in its own aura of silver above the dark blue of the sea and how, stopping in my tracks, I had ceremoniously bowed to the moon three times and wished for something nice to happen. I chose to think the acquiring of the puppy was the granting of my wish.

I rejected the name 'Glen' since it seemed to me almost every other dog in the Highlands answered to that name; also I wanted something more exclusive; something that would completely dissociate him from that smelly little box and the callousness of the debate as to his fate. I pondered as I bathed him, rubbed him dry and fed him and I was still pondering as I crossed to the barn to get some dry hay with which to stuff a cushion for his bed. As always on calm evenings at this time of year my glance lifted to the splendour of the rowan tree beside the cottage. Against the subdued colours of the autumn croft it stood like a beacon, its scarlet berries lit and its tawny foliage enflamed by the evening sunlight. I stood for a moment enjoying its brief glory, for the starlings would soon descend and strip it of its berries and my thoughts sped to the stalwart little rowan on the moors which in a different way also gave me pleasure. The right name for the puppy slid into my mind like a ticket into a slot. I called him 'Rowan'.

9

The Mirror

To my delight, when I unpacked the well-padded parcel the carrier had delivered my mirror was revealed splendidly intact save for a slight chip on the wooden frame which, since it would be futile to complain to the senders, would have to be disguised with a touch of varnish. It was no problem to hang a mirror on the stout wood-lined walls of a croft cottage so finding a nail of suitable robustness and size I hammered it in firmly and hung the mirror opposite the window where it would reflect the changing light from the wide sky and the sea. The following evening, as I half expected, there was a steady trickle of callers to inspect my new purchase but though they all exclaimed over it with well-practised enthusiasm I was nevertheless aware of some disapprobation of the mirror being positioned where it made it difficult to avoid catching a glimpse of oneself when one came into the kitchen or even when one only peered in through the window. It was not that anyone was particularly dismayed by his or her reflection; indeed the irrepressible Janet stood for a full minute roaring with laughter at her own image, but to some of the older people the possession of a mirror of such size indicated narcissism while to the excessively devout it was a vanity and as such condemned by their religion and so for their sakes, they hinted obliquely, even a doomed heretic like myself should have the consideration to keep the mirror discreetly in my bedroom.

'I think it's lovely. It really cheers up the room,' proclaimed Sheila, the young girl from Glasgow whom Tearlaich had earlier described as being 'a fine lassie right enough'. She smiled and her smile took on an extra glow as she caught Lachy looking at her in the mirror. She and Lachy had arrived together, no doubt having decided that to join what had by now become a snug ceilidh was preferable to a privacy which could be achieved only by ignoring and not escaping the inhospitably wet and blustery weather outside. Looking at their flushed cheeks and shining eyes, I found myself thinking what a pity it was that the custom of 'bundling' which used to be practised in the Hebrides as in other remote parts of the country had now died out, for quaint as it sounds, it was certainly an effective if not wholly satisfying method of ensuring for young lovers all the privacy they so much desired. In those more rigorous and perhaps more enlightened days the young couple were put to bed together on winter evenings where they might safely do their courting since the girl was first 'bundled', that is wrapped from waist to feet in strong linen cloth which was then sewn with equally strong linen thread presumably in an identifiable pattern of stitching. Nowadays, though it was easy enough in summer to find seclusion among the corries and caves on the moors, in winter Bruach lovers found any sort of privacy virtually unattainable. Croft houses which often comprised no more than a kitchen with a recessed bed and one bedroom were hardly big enough to accommodate the family let alone provide secluded corners: barns were packed roof high and tight to bursting with hay: cow byres were occupied by cows and, even ignoring the smell, were no expedient as trysting places since they were likely to be so cramped not only was one likely to step straight into animal dung immediately one opened the door but additionally there was rarely a space where one could insert oneself to avoid being copiously splashed with excrement and urine. Excellent though these are reckoned to be as a fertilizer for potatoes, it is doubtful if they could be expected similarly to nurture romance.

Clearly love could and did find a way, as was manifested by the number of children born out of wedlock in Bruach, but one felt that many of such couplings must have been urgent and uncomfortable affairs. Morag once confided to me that when one of her young men came courting they used to creep into the shed where her uncle stabled his horse. The shed was perilously near the house but the uncle and his wife were both old and 'deaf as the rocks' according to Morag, so she and her lover used to coax the horse out of the stable and tie it outside to a post. With a good feed of corn to keep it happy the horse did not object too noisily to being ousted from its warm bed which the lovers then temporarily appropriated. When the time came for the young man to return home they put the horse back into the shed, but since her uncle was only deaf and not blind, Morag and her lover had then to shovel up every vestige of manure the horse had dropped outside and place it in an acceptable position behind the horse, a task which since they dared not use a light must have been slightly more difficult than it sounds.

I looked up smiling into the mirror, unintentionally intercepting the sidelong look of love between Sheila and Lachy. Ruari, noticing the direction of my glance, was ready with his thrust. 'Aye, I doubt you will be after wantin' to make yourself look like one of those fillum stars we see in the paper now that you have your mirror,' he said.

I grinned complacently. The mirror had been bought to improve the appearance of my room but all the same I hoped it would have the effect of prodding me into giving more attention to my own appearance, which, regrettably, residence in Bruach with its devastating storms, its lack of running water, its unpredictability of supplies and consequently the plethora of excuses it offered, had encouraged me to neglect most shamefully. When I paid one of my infrequent visits to the town I was conscious that I looked more like a tinker than a crofter, for a crofter, though he cares little what he wears when he is within the bounds of his own village, ensures that he is at his smartest and well-polished best when he favours the town with a visit.

'We'll be seeing the difference on you, surely,' Janet twitted with a saucy glint in her eye. Janet was in the enviable position of never having had to take pains over her appearance. Even at the age of sixty her eyes were wide and clear and alert; her hair had no trace of grey and the fine bone structure of her face was still cleanly outlined by a perfect skin. Indeed most of the Bruach women, hard-working and burden-bearing as they had always been, were nevertheless well endowed with beauty. Of the young and the more mature almost all were possessed of flawless complexions, clear eyes and luxuriantly glossy hair, while even the very old, though their bodies may have been bent and their hands coarsened by toil and though their features may have shed the last traces of earlier beauty, had yet such a radiant serenity that, to me at any rate, it appeared a desirable supplantation.

'I certainly hope you will be seeing a difference in me,' I promised Janet. 'I got such a shock when I saw myself full-length for the first time in years I resolved to do something about it.'

Ruari handed me his empty cup and reached in his pocket for his pipe. 'I mind the first mirror ever to come to Bruach,' he announced.

'Aye, I mind about that too,' supported Morag. 'I was no more than a wee one at the time an' so you must have been yourself,' she accused Ruari.

Ruari acknowledged her accusation with a spectral nod. 'I mind just the same,' he insisted. 'It was old Peggy Beag that used to live over in Dhrinen that got it.' He waved away my offer of a refilled cup and cleared his throat.

The light from the pressure lamp was fading, indicating that the lamp needed re-pumping to bring it up to full brilliance, but I did not get up to attend to it. There was clearly a tale in the offing and tales are better told in shadow than in light. I settled more comfortably on my chair with Rowan in my lap.

'As I was after sayin', it was Peggy Beag that got the mirror from the laird that was here at the time,' Ruari began. 'Her that was the daughter of Alistair Johnny an' she married yon fellow from Glasgow. She lived in Glasgow with him for only a wee while till the fellow gave her two sons an' no more than a twelve month between them. But before the young one was more than a few months old the fellow she was married to went an' died on her. She came back to her father's croft then till he died an' the croft was her own. Ach, but livin' only a wee whiley in Glasgow had spoiled her for these parts. She'd brought some of her fancy furniture with her an' she was for puttin' up curtains at the window.' Here Ruari flicked a contemptuous glance at the curtains which framed the window of my kitchen. 'An' she was after puttin' cushions on the bench to soften it against folks' backs, so she said,' he resumed with increasing sarcasm. I could never be sure whether Ruari disapproved of curtains because he regarded them as fripperies and as such a waste of good money or because he considered them an insult to the Lord who gave light, but I could understand his contempt for cushioned comfort since it was obvious he expected the Heaven he would go to when he died would be such a bleak and comfortless place he believed in preparing for it by inuring himself to discomfort on earth.

'Now these two bairns of Peggy's was named Alistair an' Johnny,' he went on. 'An' Alistair grew up a fine strong lad as ever you'd see, with red hair and broad shoulders on him an' not wantin' in sense either. But Johnny now he was thin an' weakly an' no clever at all. What we would call hereabouts "a laugh of a lad". The two brothers had the same red hair an' were like enough to look at in other ways but ach, there was a world of difference between them even to their mother. Peggy Beag spoke only of Alistair as "my son". When she spoke of poor Johnny it was always "the laddie". Well, when he was round about seventeen years of age didn't Alistair the strong one of the two go an' catch pneumony an' in no time at all it seemed he was dead of it. Ah, Dear God! It was a terrible blow to poor Peggy Beag to lose her best son like that an' indeed there was not a one in Bruach that didn't feel sore for her loss. If it had been Johnny now that could never have been much of a support to her she wouldn't have felt the need to grieve so much, but for Alistair to be taken . . .' Ruari shook his head and stared sadly at the fire for a few moments before continuing, 'Now when the laird got to hear of Peggy's loss he goes to visit her and he says to her how sorry he is and while he's there he sees how fine she's after makin' her home. Thinkin' of some way to kind of ease her grief, he tells her that one of the bedrooms at the Big House is bein' redecorated and new furnishin's comin' and seein' he wouldn't be needin' a nice wardrobe that was there would Peggy like it for her bedroom. He would send it out on the estate cart and two of his men would come to lift it into the house for her so there would be no trouble to herself. Peggy was that pleased with him she didn't know what to say to thank him, though she did mind to ask him not to tell a soul, not even the two men that was to bring the wardrobe until it was in the cart. The laird agrees to say nothin' of it and asks her what day she wants it brought to her. Now Peggy was knowin' that the day after the next day was to be the sheep-dippin' and all the men would be away from the village and with the men all away the women would take the chance of a good ceilidh in one of the houses.' Ruari paused to slide a challenging glance at the women present. 'Peggy says to the laird that that's the day she would like the wardrobe brought seein' she wanted to keep quiet about it until she felt the wish to say something herself. When the day came the men all went off to the dippin' includin' Johnny, "the laugh of a lad", and soon enough the women were getting together at Anna Bheag's mother's house for their ceilidh so the village was as quiet as ever it could be for the cart to come with the wardrobe an' for the two men to lift it into Peggy's house. But the wardrobe when it came was very near as big as the house itself and the men were after greetin' and girnin' with the struggle they had to get it through the door. Then when Peggy said she was wantin' it in the room where she had her bed they told her there was no way else but to saw the wardrobe in half first. Peggy wasn't for havin' her fine wardrobe touched, so she told them to put it against the wall beside the dresser just, facin' the window and the door as you'd go into the house. Proud she was of it indeed and when the men had gone she set to work cleanin' and polishin'. It was a fine wardrobe right enough, carved fancy as lace on a bonnet and with a mirror on the door that was bigger even than Miss Peck-witt's just.' Ruari nodded in the direction of the mirror but avoided looking into it. 'When Peggy was content with her cleanin' and polishin' off she went to Anna Bheag's mother's house where at that time she knew most of the women would be gathered together. Wasn't my own mother one that was there and wasn't it herself that was after tellin' me the story more times than one?' testified Ruari, as if he suspected we doubted his story. 'Peggy was thinkin' to say nothin' about her wardrobe until she would be leavin' the ceilidh when she would let slip a wee mention of it and set the women to wishin' maybe they were like herself to have such a fine thing in their house. When the dusk began to show itself the women knowin' their men would soon be home from the hill were stirrin' themselves to get back and make up the fire and put on the potatoes ready, when suddenly the door of Anna Bheag's mother's house is flung open and there stands Johnny, white as the snow on the hills and shakin' with the fear that's on him. "Cailleach! Cailleach! Come quick! Come quick!" he shouts. "Alistair himself is back from the grave."

'"Alistair!" shrieks Peggy Beag, and is like to faint only for my mother keepin' a hold of her.

'"Aye right enough it's Alistair," Johnny tells her. "I swear to it; an' my God!, but he's lookin' terrible thin an' wasted with the time he's been in the grave."

'Some of the women I believe was so feared when they heard what Johnny had to say they couldn't speak just. But my own mother was not so feared. "Away with you, Alistair!" that is what she told me she said to him. "Away with you! Upsettin' your mother with your fancies. You're after bein' mistaken surely."

'"Indeed I swear to God I am no'," says Johnny. "It is true enough. True as I'm here myself at this minute. Come an' see for yourself. I seen him standing there an' he was lookin' straight at me."

'Peggy had come to herself a wee bitty by now. "My son!" she shouts and rushes out of the house followed by Johnny an' the rest of the women. When they got to the Breeshtie they found the men gathered having a last word about the days dippin' before they would be goin' back to their homes. When Johnny told them what he had seen and his voice so strong with the certainty of it they all followed Peggy to her house. When they got there they held back, an' even Peggy herself looked too feared to go in an' face whatever it was Johnny had seen. Then after a while Peggy steps out. "Am I to be feared of my own son then?" says she. "Come, Johnny!" an' pullin' Johnny after her she flings open the door. There in the light from the door she sees herself in the mirror of the wardrobe that was put in only that day for her. There's not a sign of Alistair nor even of the ghost of Alistair. She pushes Johnny in front of her. "Where did you see my son?" she says to him an' poor Johnny, still quakin' like a bog, stares at the mirror an' points to his own likeness standin' there behind her. "There," says he. As soon as Peggy Beag realized what it was she was that mad with him she nearly threw him from her. "How can you mistake your poor wee self for my own fine son?" she says to Johnny an' begins to keen for Alistair as if he'd passed on that day just.' Ruari shook his head sadly. 'Aye, you couldn't blame her for that either, but it took Johnny long enough to get over the fright he'd had an' longer even than that to get used to the mirror at all. See, it was the first mirror he'd seen an' I don't believe he ever took to it. Indeed I mind when his mother died the first thing Johnny did once she was safe in her grave was to throw stones at the mirror until it was smashed in so many pieces it lay like frost on the ground. Then he swept it up an' buried it out on the moor some place an' I believe if you dug at the hole you would be findin' some of it there to this day,' concluded Ruari. He knocked out his pipe, ran his thumb round the empty bowl and put it into his pocket, after which he sat gazing into the fire as if recalling the events with the clarity of personal involvement, though as Morag had already pointed out Ruari could not have been more than a child at the time, so it was his mother's vivid recounting of the events that he was recollecting in such detail. Thus the memories were handed down. The young people present tonight would after hearing the story no doubt add it to their own repertoire for narration when they had achieved the venerability of age.

All this time the puppy had been asleep in my lap, twitching every now and then into semi-wakefulness but always nestling back again. Erchy, who along with several others had slid unobtrusively into the ceilidh during the evening, gestured towards it. 'Aye, they like somewhere warm,' he observed.

'Show me the animal that doesn't,' Tearlaich said. 'I mind now when I was with Duncan one day when we caught a stoat. I thought the thing would tear the finger off him just but Duncan just opened his shirt and popped the beast under his vest quick as I don't know what.'

'A stoat!' I repeated incredulously. 'A wild one?'

'Aye,' insisted Tearlaich. 'Where would you find the stoat that isn't wild?'

'But didn't it bite him?' I had once seen a dog whose nose had been bitten by a stoat and the bite had been viciously deep.

'That's what I was after askin' myself,' replied Tearlaich. 'But Duncan was sayin' he'd done the same thing plenty times before and not been bitten yet. He says as soon as a stoat feels the warmth of a man's flesh it stops bein' vicious an' settles down gentle as a dove. Duncan reckons he can do the same with any beast he catches,' he added.

'He'd best not try it wiss tse bull,' quipped Hector.

'Ach, but that Duncan has so much hair on his chest the stoat would be after thinkin' it was his own nest surely,' said Morag.

Sheila gave an exaggerated shudder. 'I shouldn't like to try putting a stoat inside my vest,' she said. 'I'd be sure he'd try to bite.'

There was an unusually bright glint in Tearlaich's eye as he threw a lazy glance at Sheila's ample bosom which, constrained as it was beneath a snowy white sweater, looked like a miniature ski slope. 'I doubt you'd find room for a caterpillar inside your vest, let alone a stoat,' he told her pointedly. Sheila tittered and blushed and in trying to look demurely up at Lachy caught him staring so fixedly at her bosom that it seemed as if he at any rate was preparing to take a bite out of it. She pushed him away with a gently reproving hand.

Rowan roused himself at last and tried to jump down from my lap. I knew what he wanted, and picking him up carried him outside. The blustery wind had now given way to a breeze which was sending gusty whispers round the end of the house and as I stood in the shelter of the doorway the full moon broke cover from behind the hill and ridding itself of its cloudy beard, stayed poised, silver and serene in the dark sky.

'He'll be growin' up soft will that dog,' warned Ruari when I returned to my chair. He gave a disparaging look at the puppy which with tiny tail-wagging curiosity was now investigating the boots of the assembled company and, finding the collar of dung which trimmed Ruari's boots much to his liking, he began to lick eagerly.

'Not too soft,' I assured Ruari as I restored the puppy to my lap. I fully intended that Rowan should be well behaved and obedient, since a dog which is neither is not only a liability but it can never attain to being the trusted companion which is what I wanted Rowan to become. I realized that training would sometimes entail firmness on my part but collies are such intelligent dogs that I hoped his response would come through quick perception and understanding of my requirements rather than be merely an insensitive compliance with commands. To him I wanted to try to measure up to 'a dog's ideal of what God should be', and meanwhile I was quite unashamed of the fuss I was making of him.

In Bruach the dogs were all working dogs; either collies for sheep and cattle or cairns for rabbiting or ratting and, though there were one or two of the crofters who, deplorably, regarded their dogs as being expendable, to be worked to death and then easily disposed of with a bullet, on the whole the Bruachites treated their dogs kindly. Many were undoubtedly fond of their animals but, because it was considered the height of eccentricity to show affection for a dog, the owners, when they knew they were being observed, felt they had to speak brusquely and sometimes appear to behave almost callously towards them. Very rarely a crofter would defy the gibes and sarcasm and openly display affection for his dog. One such was an old bachelor who, when he could no longer look after himself, came from a neighbouring village with his much-loved dog to spend his last days in Bruach with a married sister. The old man had cancer and as his illness progressed and he became too weak to exercise his dog he had to rely on a nephew to do this for him. Now the old man's dog, though it could not be described as an aggressive animal, had a strange habit whenever it saw another dog of rushing towards it and leaping clean over it, after which display of exhuberance it would continue indifferently on its way. The village dogs being on the whole tolerant and sensible animals quickly learned, or were commanded to lie down when they became aware of the approach of the old man's dog and so life for the canine population continued placidly. However, one day the nephew had the dog down by the cliffs when it espied another dog and oblivious of the fact that the other dog was crouching by the edge of the cliff it made its customary rush forward and a moment later leaped to its death a hundred feet below on the rocky shore. When the nephew returned home the old man naturally wanted to know why the dog was not with him and the nephew, reluctant to give him the bad news, pretended at first that the dog had gone after a bitch and would soon be home. But the old man had become increasingly perturbed by its absence and eventually he had to be told the truth. He died that night.

'Right enough we knew he'd got to die but the doctor reckoned he had a whiley yet,' the nephew declared. 'But ach, when I told him about the dog I seen the life go out of his eyes even supposin' it didn't leave the rest of his body. Then next mornin' we found him gone an' his hand hangin' down beside the bed like as if he was reachin' to pat his dog that had always slept on the mat beside him.'

Erchy turned to Tearlaich. 'I didn't see your own dog for a whiley,' he said. 'Have you got him tied up for something?'

'Ach, he's got himself a bad leg,' Tearlaich replied. 'I reckon he's put it out of joint tryin' to lift it higher than all the other dogs in Bruach.'

'Indeed I don't wonder your dog has a bad leg,' said Erchy. 'The way he runs when you send him after the sheep, you'd think he had nothing but the wind inside him. I'm thinkin' if you took him anywhere near a town they would be finin' him for exceeding the speed limit.'

'He's fast but he's no bad at the sheep,' conceded Tearlaich. 'But he barks too much an' he likes fine if he gets the chance to take a wee nip at their heels every now and then, though I belt him for it if I can get near him.'

'I don't think much of a dog that nips,' said Ruari, getting up to go. 'Nor one that would be barkin' at them too much. A nice quiet dog is what you need for the hill.'

'You want a dog like the one a famous writer is supposed to have said was his ideal,' I told them and quoted, '"Wanted a dog that neither barks nor bites but eats broken glass and shits diamonds."'

Tearlaich flashed me a look from under raised brows. 'My dog wouldn't be much good to that fellow,' he speculated. 'He both barks and bites but he eats fishbones and shits glue.'

The pressure lamp began to 'pop' repeatedly,

indicating its urgent need of pumping, and since it would fill the kitchen with the smell of smoke and paraffin if I let it go out I got up to attend to it. In the resulting brightness I noticed that Sheila and Lachy had disappeared and that the chair they had been sharing was now occupied by Erchy. I had not noticed the couple leave but since the weather had so much improved I surmised they had slipped out discreetly and gone to some secluded spot where they might pursue their pleasure safe from the teasing comments of onlookers. I looked enquiringly at Morag and she nodded amused affirmation.

'It's still quite chilly outside,' I murmured, shrugging my shoulders to chase out the nippy cold which had struck them while I was waiting for Rowan.

'Aye, but I daresay they're warm enough where they are now,' said Erchy, and his remark was greeted with a chorus of giggles. He winked heavily at me.

Soon after Ruari had gone there was a shuffle of boots and calls of 'Oidhche mhath!' as the rest of the company told one another they ought to be going home.

'Well, mho ghaoil, I've fairly enjoyed my ceilidh,' said Morag when only the two of us were left. I too had enjoyed the ceilidh, for now that I had become more integrated into the crofting way of life I invariably enjoyed any ceilidh into which I was drawn and since there were only three sources of entertainment in Bruach – ceilidhing, copulating and church-going – perhaps it was well that I did.

The Bruachites used the word 'ceilidh' to describe any sort of indoor meeting whether it was merely a tête-à-tête or whether it was in the nature of a social gathering, and their use of the term was understandable since the one frequently developed into the other. If I dropped in on Morag of an evening for a chat we had a 'wee ceilidh' but it required only one or two people to be observed visiting a house for that house to become a magnet for more visitors and so to the satisfaction of everyone a true ceilidh resulted. Thus Bruach ceilidhs were always spontaneous, whereas in many other villages ceilidhs were held in halls instead of homes and not only were they prearranged and advertised but the audience were required to sit on ncat rows of chairs. Such contrived gatherings would hardly have suited Bruach where the best ceilidhing was always to be found in the cosier houses, that is where the woman was not especially houseproud and had no fancy ideas about precious furniture that might be spoiled and where people were left to adjust themselves as they liked according to the space available. I well recall Morag's reaction when, as we were driving through a mainland village, she spotted a notice announcing a ceilidh. So disapproving was she that she asked me to stop the car so she could get out and read it. 'And they have a fear an tighe too,' she said, her mouth bent with disapproval. She got back into the car. 'Likely it's a bit of Glasgow swank they're puttin' on,' she excused them.

'It seems odd having to announce a ceilidh even in such a small village,' I said.

'Indeed, but there's some places would be needin' to put up a notice that there is water in the well,' Morag returned derisively.

She went out into the night and returning to the kitchen I gave Rowan his supper of bread and milk and, so I should not need to go outside again after taking my own nightcap of hot milk and biscuits, I ushered him towards the door. But instead of coming out into the porch he stopped at the kitchen door and looking up at me expectantly began wagging his tail excitedly. I tried to think of a cause for his excitement. Sometime during the ceilidh, presumably because the heat of the fire and the number of bodies present had caused the kitchen to become too hot, the door had been opened wide back against the wall where it had stayed for the rest of the evening and, remembering that I had earlier that day made a toy for the puppy from a duster tied with string, I assumed the toy had somehow lodged itself behind the door and the puppy was now intent on retrieving it. I pulled the door away from the wall.

'You!' I gasped, and for the moment that was all I could say. Astonishingly love had found a way, for there in the small wedge of space between the open door and the wall stood Sheila and Lachy, now releasing themselves from a tight and sweaty embrace and giggling unashamedly at my discovery of them. This then was where the couple had disappeared to earlier in the evening and suddenly recollecting Erchy's remark and its accompanying wink I realized it was only I who had been ignorant of the fact. Whether they had been too absorbed to notice the departure of the rest of the company or whether they were hoping I would go to my bed without discovering them I do not know but they were in no way abashed as they bade me an exultant farewell.

As the sound of their mutual teasing and chuckling receded, I closed the door and leaned back against the support of the staircase, ready to give way to the laughter which was already beginning to dispel my initial consternation.

Rowan piddled on the mat as he waited.

10

Christmas Sabbath

'How's life?' I greeted Erchy and Tearlaich as we waited along with a disordered queue of Bruachites for our turn to be served at the weekly grocery van.

'Ach, no bad,' said Erchy.

'Pretty good,' said Tearlaich. 'Mind I have to

complain a bit at times but only enough to show good manners just.'

'Who's complainin'?' asked Morag, stepping down from the van and stuffing loaves of wrapped bread into a flour sack. 'Indeed you men is always after findin' somethin' to be girnin' about.'

Tearlaich looked resigned. 'I wasn't complainin' for one,' he repudiated.

'I'm feelin' like doin' some complainin' then,' said Erchy.

'An' what would be upsettin' you?' Morag asked.

'Not what but who,' Erchy told her. 'It's that man Shamus Mor that's upsettin' me.'

'Shamus Mor? Angus Ruag's half-brother?'

'Himself.' Erchy nodded.

'Ach, that man,' said Morag. 'You're no tellin' me he's back again?'

'He is so,' said Erchy, and directed at me a fragmentary wink in recognition of shared knowledge.

'Well indeed, but Bruach was well rid of that man when he took himself off,' declaimed Morag. 'They tell me he's been hoppin' about since like a hen on a hot girdle; Australia an' Canada an' the Dear knows where an' never stayin' more than a wee whiley in any one place.'

'Well, he'll be stayin' where he's goin' now,' said Erchy positively, and when she turned to him with a sceptical expression he announced exultantly, 'He's dead!'

'Dead?' echoed Morag. 'Why did I no' hear of it then?'

'Because you were too taken up with that woman that's stayin' with Janet, likely,' Erchy retorted.

'Indeed wasn't all the women there? We took a look in at the window an' you were listenin' to her as keen as if she was after tellin' you where you would find a cask or two of whisky.'

'What woman's that?' interpolated Tearlaich, as if the village was beset by strange women.

'Ach, the one you were sayin' yourself has the look of a heifer that's missed the bull,' Erchy reminded him.

'The diagression,' Morag elucidated.

'What's a diagression?' asked Tearlaich.

'Like a missionary,' Erchy took it upon himself to explain, 'but instead of tellin' you everythin' you do or fancy doin' is wicked she tells you everythin' you eat or want to eat is goin' to kill you.'

'Aye, indeed,' endorsed Morag. 'I believe she's wantin' us to eat grass the same as the cows.'

'Not grass,' I corrected quietly. 'Just green vegetables; cabbages and kale and things.'

'Is she still here then?' asked Tearlaich. 'I thought she was stayin' the one night just.'

'That was the way of it but her car broke somethin',' said Morag.

'Likely she's been tryin' to feed that cabbages,' suggested Erchy.

'Whisht!' Morag whispered. 'Here she comes this minute.' We composed our expressions as Janet and her guest approached.

I had already met the dietician, since I also had been one of the number of women who by open invitation had gathered at Janet's house the previous evening to listen to a talk about food and health. Whether our instructor had come in an official capacity or whether she had been prompted by her own concern for our well-being to try and persuade the Bruachites to reform their eating habits was not quite clear, but predictably, since strangers who had something to say were always welcome in Bruach, there was a fair gathering of women prepared to listen. As we expected, she advised eating more green vegetables, something which I certainly aspired to do. But how to obtain them? The answer came glibly: grow them, of course! A small patch of the croft would provide plenty of vegetables for a family. Why yes, indeed, the women agreed, turning to look at each other with pretended surprise as if this was the first time the suggestion had been put to them; as if they had not given up trying to grow them in the teeth of storms and the ravages of the cattle; as if they had not proved repeatedly that their families spurned green vegetables, even supposing they were able to procure them. But the Bruachites, making no attempt to disillusion her, listened with an interest which though feigned was tolerably convincing. For a time I was attentive to much of what she had to say, but unfortunately the woman was afflicted with a voice that whined on all evening, plaguing as draught through a keyhole, and growing restless I made my excuses and left early. It was my leaving early that had led to my being one jump ahead of Morag with the news of Shamus Mor's death, for on my way home I had met Erchy who had just received a message from the undertaker.

'He fooar!' Janet greeted us as she and her visitor reached the van. There was a reciprocal chorus of,

'He fooars!' but almost before they had rumbled away the 'diagression' had pounced on Morag's sack of loaves.

'Oh, my dear, but surely no family can eat that amount of bread in a week? It's most unhealthy,' she began, and then she saw Anna Beag coming away from the van with several packs of biscuits protruding from the top of her sack. 'And biscuits!' she wailed, as if the sight of them was a personal affront. She assessed the waiting customers as if selecting more victims for her advice and the several bachelors who were shopping for their own needs were conscientious in their efforts to appear otherwise occupied. Undeterred, the 'diagression', figuratively taking the centre of the stage, began haranguing us on our eating habits; and now the presence of men in the audience encouraged her to hold forth not only on food but also on the lethal effects of whisky and pipe-smoking. Some of the men looked startled; others rammed their empty pipes into their mouths so as to conceal their contemptuous smiles.

When she had finished there was an embarrassed lull for some minutes and then Erchy said sombrely, 'Come to think of it, livin' is the unhealthiest thing we do; we all die of that sometime.'

The embarrassment was smoothed by laughter in which even the 'diagression' joined somewhat tepidly and since it was now my turn to be served I heard no more of the discussion.

Later that evening we heard that the broken car had been 'sorted' and the lady had left Bruach. At the ensuing ceilidh Janet expressed relief.

'Indeed didn't Lachlan have to go back to the van when I got home to get bread and biscuits that I didn't dare put in my poc for fear the woman would start on me again,' she said.

'I'm thinkin' the woman's daft,' observed Tearlaich casually.

'Even supposin' she was daft it makes a change to listen to her all the same,' defended Morag.

'Ach, the egg's not worth the cackle,' Murdoch summed up.

'Well, she was pleased enough with Miss Peckwitt for sayin' she baked her own bread,' pursued Katy Beag. 'An' she was after sayin' when we get the electric we would all be the better for bakin' our own bread, though when we would find the time to do it the Dear only knows,' she ended with a defiant chuckle.

'I don't like the electric,' said Morag flatly. 'There's no heart in it.'

'It's no' heart but heat you'll get from it, you silly old cailleach,' Tearlaich told her.

'No, but what I was meanin' was the light,' she explained. 'It's no like lamplight. It's that quick it makes me jump.'

'You want to be glad of anythin' that will make you jump at your age,' Tearlaich remarked searingly.

I found myself agreeing with Morag, for, though the necessarily slow lighting of an oil lamp, the initial dimness followed by the gradual turning-up of the wick, can be frustrating at times, I always felt it had the effect of politely introducing the daylight to the darkness rather than simply banishing it in a flash.

'Well, the electric's comin', like it or not,' said Erchy. 'An' I'm one that will be more than glad to see it.'

'Miss Peckwitt has tse electric already,' Hector reminded them.

Behag nudged me, directing my attention to old Donald, who, with a severely disapproving expression, was staring down at the floor.

'Only a fence,' I said, 'and that's worked by batteries.' I had purchased the electric fence on the advice of a friend who had been staying with me in the summer and who, seeing the healthy young cabbages I had managed to grow in the small sheltered plot behind the cottage, had predicted that I would have some really stout-hearted cabbages for the winter.

'Not a hope,' I told him. 'It happens year after year. I've managed to provide them with a little more shelter this year but as soon as the crofts are open to the animals in the autumn they'll break in somehow and ravage the lot.'

He had then advised me to get an electric fence, explaining that once an animal had received a shock from the live wire it would never go near it again, even supposing the current was turned off. The fence need not be particularly robust, either, he assured me in answer to one of the doubts I raised. Convinced at last by his enthusiasm, I had written off to the mainland and ordered the fence which Erchy had helped me to erect and so far I was delighted with the results. The crofts had been open for some weeks now but still my cabbages remained unmolested, partly I suspect because it was the delight of the children of Bruach to bring their cows along, push their wet noses on to the live wire and watch the cows leap away at the shock. Since the current was not strong enough to harm the cow, the children's ploy, reprehensible though it may be considered, served the dual purpose of teaching the animals respect for the fence and at the same time preserving my cabbages. But reputedly, for he had not approached me in the matter, Old Donald was extremely angry with me, not because I had an electric fence but because I allowed that fence to work on the Sabbath. Had I switched it off on Saturday night and left it switched off until Monday morning he would have accepted the fence with the same interest and curiosity as the rest of the crofters, but Donald was numbered among the excessively devout of the village. The fence offended him greatly and, since I had no intention of switching off the current as he considered I should, it continued to offend him. As a consequence, though I forbore mentioning it to the 'diagression', I still had some cabbages in my garden.

'Aye, well, once the electric comes I daresay we'll all be gettin' shocks an' jumpin' about from one place to another the same as the cows,' said Janet.

'Speakin' of shocks,' said Morag, 'did you get the grave dug yet, Erchy, for Shamus Mor?'

'I did so,' replied Erchy. 'That's just what I was sayin' earlier on when we were at the van that I had somethin' to complain about. Why would a man that's lived most of his life some place else have to be brought here when he's dead so as to make us have to dig a grave for him? It's no right, I'm tellin' you.

I was no more than a bairn when he left here so why should I have to dig his grave for him? A dead man canna give me a dram for my trouble, can he?' His voice was edged with outrage.

'He has no' much in the way of relatives left but for Barbac that's married over in Rhuna, so who else would dig his grave?' asked Morag.

'Damty sure it shouldn't be me,' said Erchy.

'Right enough, it's bad when there's no one to give you a good dram for your trouble,' sympathized Murdoch. 'But who was it asked you to dig the grave, then?'

'The undertaker himself. He got word by telephone only last night that the corpse was on its way an' he was to make all the necessary arrangements. That's what he says he was told to do.'

'Ach, then likely the undertaker will include a bottle of whisky in with the necessary arrangements,' Murdoch comforted. 'After all, he'll need it for the minister.'

'Who helped you with the diggin'?' asked Johnny. 'I couldn't get myself seein' the mails was that late.'

'Help? Indeed I did it mostly myself. Hector came for a wee while until he sprackled away after somethin' or other an' then there was young Hamish. He'd been learnin' how to kill a sheep in the mornin' so he hadn't much stomach left for diggin' a grave afterwards.' Erchy's eyes grew bright. 'I had a bit of fun with him all the same,' he told us. 'See, we'd been diggin' for a bit an' then I see we're liftin' a few bones out with the earth so I tell Hamish to put them back in. When I see he hasn't done it I look to find what he's doin' an' there's the loon pushin' the bones around an' tryin' will he lift them on his spade, as particular as if he was tryin' to lift pieces of shell out of a broken egg with a knife. "Dear God, Hamish!" I says to him. "Can you no pick them up in your fingers, he's only your grandfather." Honest! I thought the lad would be sick in the hole he was diggin' the way he looked.'

'You put Shamus Mor in the same grave with Angus Ruag that was young Hamish's grandfather?' cried Morag. 'Whatever made you do that?'

Erchy shrugged. 'Why not? They were kind of brothers, weren't they?'

Morag evaded disclosing how Angus Ruag and Shamus Mor came to be 'kind of brothers'. 'There were never two men more apart,' she explained. 'Angus Ruag was a man, a fine man; Shamus Mor was never more than a wee tick. Was it not Angus Ruag himself that carried all the turf from the moor to cover the bare rock of his croft until he could cut hay from it? My, but Angus was a warrior.'

'Aye, indeed,' Murdoch assented.

Angus Mor had been alive when I first came to live in Bruach and I recalled him well. He was 'eighty past' at that time but all the same one could detect the fine man Morag had described despite the toll of old age. I could remember him telling me with quiet dignity how, when he had first inherited his croft, it had been one of the poorest in Bruach, much of it being nothing but barren rock; he told me of how he had vowed he would set about improving it ready for his own son to inherit and how with this purpose in mind he had made the journey to the moors at least once every day no matter what other work he had to do and wherever he could find green grass from there he had cut turves which he had carried back and laid over the rock of his croft. Day after day, year after year during his long lifetime he had done this until his croft was as green as the best of the crofts in the village. Standing there looking over the land he had so laboriously imposed upon the rock he had pointed out to me the very last area to be covered, telling me of the deep satisfaction it had given him when only the previous year he had been able to cut from it the first swathes of hay. The pride in his unhurried voice was expressive of his love for and dedication to his land, for Angus Ruag had continued his self-imposed task long after the son whom he had hoped would inherit had been killed in the war.

'Well, I hope the pair will rest quiet,' said Sheena.

'Well, if they don't we'll take Miss Peckwitt's electric fence an' put it round the grave,' said Tearlaich. 'That will keep them where they belong.'

The following Monday morning Erchy, who was on his way down to his boat, popped in at the cottage to ask, 'Is your electric fence workin' all right?'

'So far as I know,' I replied. 'It was working earlier on this morning because I heard it ticking away as usual.'

'Well, Old Donald's not tickin' away as usual,' said Erchy with a mysterious smile.

The connexion between my fence and Donald leaped quite naturally to my mind. 'Has he been trying to interfere with it?' I demanded suspiciously.

'Aye, well,' Erchy began, 'you know the way he

feels about your fence workin' on the Sabbath? Well, me an' some of the boys was at his house ceilidhin' the other night an' teasin' him about it until Donald says he wished he knew of a way of stoppin' the fence workin' just for the Sabbath like, not spoilin' it altogether, mind. So Tearlaich winks at me an' says he knows a way. "What way is that?" says Donald, so Tearlaich tells him. "Are you sure it will work?" says he. "Sure as I'm here," Tearlaich tells him, so on Saturday night me an' the boys follow Donald to your croft an' wait to see him set about putting your fence out of action.'

'What did he do?' I snapped.

'He did what Tearlaich told him to do, just,' said Erchy. 'He peed on it.'

I stared at him aghast. 'He did what?'

Erchy's expression was one of sheer joy. 'He did what I said he did.'

'Good gracious!' I ejaculated. 'Tearlaich's a fiend. What happened?'

Erchy blushed. 'You'll have to be findin' that out for yourself,' he told me, beginning to move away, and to save him further embarrassment I restrained myself from pointing out the patent impossibility of my ever being able to find out for myself. 'I'll tell you one thing, though,' he flung over his shoulder as he went, 'for the first time anyone can remember Old Donald wasn't in church yesterday.'

'I hope he's all right,' I called after him.

'Ach, he's all right. He just got a wee bitty shock, that's all,' he called back.

Remembering Donald's tackety boots, I suspected he might have got more than 'a wee bitty shock'.

I mentioned the incident to Morag later in the week when I met her on my way up to the Post Office.

'The crazy bodach!' she said with a delighted chuckle.

'If you ever find out what happened to him do tell me, won't you?' I coaxed. But she only laughed again and I guessed she and probably the rest of the village were by now well aware of what had happened to Donald. It was only I who was destined to remain in ignorance. I still feel a little excluded that I do not know what happens to an old man when he pees on a live electric wire but unless someone enlightens me I suppose I shall have to go on feeling that way.

Morag had a dead cockerel swinging from either hand and we were soon joined by Anna Vic who was also carrying a couple of cockerels, for it was only ten days before New Year and the killing and the posting-off of cockerels to relatives and friends in the city was the most easily detectable sign of its approach. Ten days to New Year meant only three days to Christmas and since I now had too many commitments to think of leaving the croft and going down to England for the holiday I knew that I should be spending Christmas alone – alone that is except for Rowan, who by this time was well grown and sturdy enough to accompany me wherever my wanderings took me. This he did happily, instinctively staying at my side unless I bade him do otherwise. There were other things he did instinctively and one of them was herding my chickens. Whenever I was working in or around the cottage and therefore he could be satisfied I was not in need of protection, Rowan, while never going out of sight, liked to take himself off to the shed where I had a brood of chickens not long deserted by the mother hen. There he would begin quietly and gently rounding up the chickens as if they were sheep before herding them into the shed. Once he had them penned in the shed he would go inside and send them all out again ready to resume herding them once more. It is said that poultry are difficult to herd, since unlike sheep they do not flock naturally and also they have wings as well as legs to enable them to elude the herder and it was fascinating to watch the way Rowan worked them. His approach was stealthy, never panicking the chickens and one could almost detect his brain working out the strategy he would have to use to bring a straying chick or two back to the flock without scattering the rest. Round and round the shed, he prowled and stalked and shuffled, infinitely patient, until he had worn a track in the grass which I would have sworn was a perfect circle, and every taut muscle, every hair of his coat as well as the gleam in his eye proclaimed his rapturous absorption in his play. Round and round and in and out of the shed the chickens ran, or flew or hopped, evidencing no enjoyment whatsoever of their enforced activity but only a dazed compliance with Rowan's relentless shepherding. I sometimes wondered whether it was good for chickens to be so frequently harassed but I need not have worried. By the time they had reached maturity they may have been the longest-legged chickens which had ever been seen in Bruach but they were by far the best layers I had ever had in my flock.

'My, but those are good birds you have there, Morag,' Anna Vic complimented, gesturing towards Morag's cockerels.

'They're good birds you have yourself,' Morag returned. 'They will be for your daughter, likely?'

'They are so,' admitted Anna Vic. 'She was sayin' to send them a day or two earlier this year because last year they didn't get them till New Year's Eve an' there was barely time to pluck an' clean the beasts before they was wantin' to be eatin' them. But will they keep, only the Dear knows.'

'They'll keep surely,' Morag said. 'Seein' you didn't pluck them.'

In Bruach it was reckoned that a plucked and drawn fowl would not keep fresh nearly so long as one which had not been opened up in any way. They were 'airtight' they believed and it was the custom to send cockerels through the post with their necks wrung but unplucked, undrawn and even unwrapped, with just a label tied to their legs to indicate their destination.

Morag swung one of the birds out of the way of Rowan, who, being puzzled by the inactivity of the dead birds, was following with his nose close to their beaks as if he expected them to need rounding up at any moment. 'This one is for my cousin that's the detecertive in Glasgow,' she told us, 'him that was here with his wife in the summer, you mind?'

'Indeed I mind,' said Anna Vic. 'It was good ceilidhin' we had then with all the tales he had to tell of the pollis an' the rogues they're after catchin'.'

She glanced at Morag. 'Maybe we'll be seein' them back this comin' summer yet.'

'I doubt we will,' said Morag. 'His letter was sayin' his wife's no better.'

'Is she ill?' It was I who asked the question and with some surprise since the wife had appeared to be such a healthy little woman; effervescing with fun and delightful company.

'Surely, mo ghaoil, did I no' tell you she had gone malignant?' Morag replied. 'The doctor's after givin' her injections but I doubt she'll be well enough in time to come this next year.'

'I'm truly sorry to hear it,' I said. 'Please remember me to them both when next you write.'

Anna Vic said, 'That puts me in mind of your own friend that was in hospital. Is she better now?'

'Mary's coming out of hospital today,' I told her. 'She'll be going home for Christmas. That's why I'm going to the Post Office now. I'm going to send her some flowers to cheer her up.'

Morag turned to me with a puzzled look. 'But, mo ghaoil,' she reasoned, 'where now would you be gettin' flowers at this time of year? An' if you could get a hold of them where would you find anyone that would take them to her?'

I smiled. 'I'm going to send them by Interflora,' I explained. 'It's an organization which enables you to order flowers, say, from a shop in Inverness and have them delivered by a shop close to where the recipient lives.'

'Interflora?' mused Morag. 'That's handy right enough.'

'It is,' I agreed. 'I use it quite a lot.'

By this time we had arrived at the Post Office and while I filled in a telegraph form Morag and Anna Vic added their cockerels to the pile which was already spilling over from the large mailbag in the corner. Before we had finished our business Tearlaich and Hector appeared in the doorway.

'Ah, New Year's comin' closer,' gloated Tearlaich. 'I always like to see the cockerels goin' off at this time of year because then I know I haven't long to wait to start gettin' drunk.' He and Hector grinned at each other, their eyes already lit with New Year anticipation.

'You get drunk plenty times,' Anna Vic said.

'Aye but not New Year drunk,' refuted Tearlaich. 'Not bloody, blind mad drunk the way we can be then. Dear God! But I'm goin' to enjoy myself. I was sick last year an' couldn't take a drop but I'm goin' to have two New Years in one this time.' He turned to me. 'Miss Peckwitt, I guarantee you won't see a man that's as drunk as me,' he boasted.

'He's started already rehearsin' for it,' said Hector.

'Of course I have,' Tearlaich admitted. 'Me an' Erchy reckon to go into trainin' for New Year a couple of weeks before. We don't want to waste good whisky by gettin' drunk too quickly.'

'All this talk of New Year but it's Christmas is Miss Peckwitt's time,' Morag reminded him.

'More fool her,' responded Tearlaich. 'I can never understand the fuss the English make of Christmas and yet when New Year comes they seem as if they'd sooner work than drink.' He gave me a commiserating glance. 'All the same, it's a shame you haven't more of your own folk around to celebrate with.'

'Even supposin' she could get away she couldn't stay with her friend seein' she's only newly out of hostapol,' Morag told him.

'Is that true?' he asked. I nodded. 'In that case she'll not be havin' much of a Christmas herself then,' he said with polite concern.

'No indeed but hasn't Miss Peckwitt just been tellin' me she's after sendin' someone from Interpol to cheer her up with some flowers,' Morag was quick to inform him.

It was Christmas Eve – a Saturday when the evening of frosty calm allowed the purpled islands to peer down at their images in the turquoise water while distant lighthouses blinked with increasing brilliance as the last shreds of what had been a flamboyant sunset were sucked into the sea. The crofts being open to the cattle meant that we had not far to go to round up our cattle for the evening milking and the voices of women urging cows, scolding reckless dogs or children and screaming at other cows which had ventured too close rasped at the frosty silence. During the afternoon the men had been carrying home extra creels of peats and the children had been carrying extra pails of water which now stood already skimmed with ice outside the cottage but within handy reach of the door. Calves had been housed for the night; poultry had been fed and gone murmuringly to roost and except for the occasional moo of protest from a cow which had not yet been given its evening feed of hay there was virtually no other sound. It was Christmas Eve; tomorrow was Christmas Day but the preparations took no account of that. Tomorrow was the Sabbath and already by four o'clock on the Saturday afternoon, or evening as it was designated in Bruach, the Sabbath calm descended over the village like a sad grey mist.

As the sky shouldered its burden of deepening darkness, cottage windows began to glow, indicating that the womenfolk, having finished their milking and calf-feeding, had now returned to the house to resume preparations for the morrow. Batches of scones had to be baked; meat, whether it was butcher meat, a rabbit or a skart, would have to be boiled ready to be eaten cold; potatoes had to be brought in from the clamp in the barn, washed and, depending on the degree of piety of the family, either put into a pan and covered with cold water ready for cooking on the Sabbath or, as in the more inflexible households, boiled and drained ready to be eaten cold. Likewise there were eggs to be boiled and porridge or brose to be scalded and set ready by the hob. While the women worked, the children cleaned and polished the family's boots and pestered their mothers for lost socks and clean underwear. The men shaved and, if they thought they needed to, cut their toenails and fingernails and cut the children's toenails and fingernails, after which they smoked contemplatively or drank tea while they allowed the females of the family to wait on them until, work done, they could begin the evening prayers.

By five o'clock on Christmas Eve my own work outside and inside was finished. Bonny and her calf were in their stalls in the byre, their mangers topped up with hay; the hen house with its huddle of roosting hens was shut tight against the cold. Rowan and I returned to the cottage, which was already decorated with holly and ivy brought home the previous day from the sheltered little copse across the bay. There was also a bunch of pine branches threaded with tarnished tinsel which made a cheerful substitute for a Christmas tree and as I had managed to get the accumulator of my wireless set charged I was thinking I might have a pleasant if not festive evening listening to the sounds of an English Christmas even though I was deprived of the scenes. Had Christmas Day not fallen on the Sabbath I should at this time have been busily and happily baking and preparing for a children's party, but since it did there could not be the merest mention of the word 'party' and there was little I could do to dispel nostalgia save stay up to listen to the Watchnight Service and join in the singing of the carols.

In Bruach the morning of the Sabbath was always one of late rising; the day was one of boredom; of the disallowing of unnecessary toil and the total prohibition of pleasure. Even a walk on the moors or too close an approach to the shore was proscribed by the more fanatical. Bible reading and church-going were the only 'pleasures' permitted; the missionary and the minister the only callers welcome in the home.

On the Christmas Day Sabbath I slept late and

when I drew back the curtains I gasped with pleasure.

In the night the snow had come, softly and stealthily to swathe the land and now, unexpected and exciting as a white-wrapped gift, it awaited investigation. It was Rowan's first encounter with snow and he slid and pranced and capered about delightedly as I let out the hens and coaxed Bonny from the warmth of the byre. Normally I liked to bake bread on Sunday mornings, regarding it as being as satisfying a devotional exercise as going to church. But Christmas Day had to be different and once the morning feeding and milking was finished Rowan and I shuffled through the crisp snow searching for the tracks of animals which we might follow. The hills and the islands were magnificent in their new white cladding; the sea was a sun-tinted icy blue and the few clouds, tranquil as if they were slumbering in the sky, were soft and puffy with sunlit edges reminding me of fluffy suet dumplings dribbled with golden syrup. After we had been out about an hour the sky greyed briefly to release a further sprinkling of snow which descended gracefully, unhurried by even a breath of wind. It settled gently on my Burberry and on Rowan's coat and it was all so compellingly beautiful that I did not seek shelter but waited, enclosed in the stillness and the silent, dream-like quality of the falling snow. When it ceased and the sun emerged again Rowan shook himself and for a transient moment was enveloped in tiny rainbows of melted snow. The scene was exquisite; solace for all but the most persistent nostalgia and I felt smug that I was enjoying such splendour while the wireless report implied there was nothing in the English weather that was minutely enjoyable; only the misery of driving sleet and hail with slush underfoot.

The evening darkness came early and back home I noticed the barometer was falling steadily. I had hoped for a few days of calm but it seemed it was not to be, and after supper I poured myself a festive glass of wine and taking advantage of the continuing quiet stood for a few moments in the doorway of the cottage, counting my blessings. The lamp spread the snow with a fan of golden light and the wireless effused the voices of a carolling choir. But already the sky was beginning to be patched with dark, hard-looking clouds like bundles of steel wool that were scrubbing out the reflected moonlight. I closed the door and later, as I lingered over a second glass of wine and another of the mince pies I had baked the previous day I heard above the singing of the choir the first threatening whisper of wind; a whisper that was gradually augmented by a crowd of whispers which began to pick up the crisp particles of snow and fling them wantonly against the window. The crowded whispers were not long in swelling to a harsh full-throated roar and before the evening had finally yielded to the night the gale was upon us.

With doors wedged and bolstered against the penetrating draughts, curtains drawn and fire banked up I settled down to my Christmas cheer. If this wind continued to increase I knew how daunting would be the weather I should wake up to in the morning; how when I ventured outside, as I must, the cold would lacerate my face; the wind thrust against my body and tear at my breath until I was almost sobbing as I struggled against its bitter strength. But I drove such thoughts out of my mind. It had been a lovely Christmas Day, after all. And tomorrow was tomorrow!